ELEMENTAL ELEMENTALISM

ELEMENTAL
ELEMENTALISM

Elemental Elementalism

CONTENTS

ELEMENTAL FOUNDATIONS

1. THE FIRST TENET OF ELEMENTALISM

1.1.   Consciousness is the prima materia.

1.2.   This is the First and Foundational Tenet of Elementalism.

1.3.   Consciousness is the original source from which all else manifests.

1.4.   Consciousness is eternal and immutable, being outside of time and space. As such, it is the one thing whose existence needs no explanation.

1.5.   Consciousness came first, before language, before thought, before matter, even before the division into masculine and feminine or the division into good and evil.

1.6.   People today only consider consciousness a mystery because they are lost in the veils of materialism. This traps them in ludicrous misconceptions, such as the idea that the brain generates consciousness.

1.7.   The simple truth is that consciousness is more fundamental than the physical world. It existed for an eternity before the physical world first manifested, and will exist for an eternity after the physical world unmanifests.

1.8. Because consciousness is more fundamental than language, it cannot be described in language. As such, there are no definitions of consciousness that make any sense.

1.9. Anyone who is conscious knows what consciousness is, and therefore can understand it without a definition.

1.10. The Elementalist doesn't try to define consciousness. The assumption is that anyone trying to define it doesn't understand it.

1.11. Elementalism teaches that materialism is to ontology what Flat Earth Theory is to astronomy. Every Elementalist understands that materialism is a primitive theory for those who don't get it.

1.12. The idea that consciousness evolved from biological processes of natural and sexual selection will, one enlightened day, be categorised alongside the idea that the Moon is made of cheese.

1.13. Consciousness has always existed, since before there were even bacteria on Earth, because consciousness dreamed up the Earth, and not the other way around.

1.14. The Elementalist knows that consciousness is the primary and foundational element of all those that exist. All else is dependent upon it.

1.15. Consciousness, in its creative infinity, is the same thing as God.

1.16. The consciousness possessed by the individual is an infinitely small fragment of the total glory possessed by God.

1.17. All of us who are conscious (which is all of us) are God.

1.18. The average Westerner is conditioned to believe that physical matter is the prima materia, and that their own consciousness is something that evolved out of ever-complexifying self-reproducing organic forms.

1.19. Knowing consciousness to be the prima materia, the Elementalist is unafraid of death, recognising the death of one's body to merely be a change of physical form.

1.20. Because consciousness is the prima materia, all else is mere perception, which rises and falls like the wind. That which perceives remains resolute in eternity.

1.21. An Elementalist can immediately overcome any death anxiety by recalling the First Tenet.

1.22. Meditating regularly upon the First Tenet will build a spiritual armour that defends from any fears grounded in biology or materialism.

1.23. The one who meditates regularly upon the First Tenet will know that all of the horrors of this world are nothing more than the illusion of threat, and their combined power is nothing more than the ability to alter perception.

1.24. Understanding the First Tenet leads naturally to the Second Tenet.

2. THE SECOND TENET OF ELEMENTALISM

2.1. The Conceivable Universe is divided into consciousness and the Great Fractal.

2.2. This is the Second and Divisional Tenet of Elementalism.

2.3. The First Tenet of Elementalism is that consciousness is the prima materia. The Second Tenet relates to the division of this prima materia, which is the division of consciousness into consciousness and the Great Fractal.

2.4. In the beginning, consciousness is only conscious of itself. But by willingly choosing to forget parts of itself, it can cause itself to become conscious of other things.

2.5. All of these other things, whether physical or metaphysical, make up the Great Fractal, which itself is everything that it is possible for consciousness to perceive or to conceive of.

2.6. The Conceivable Universe, then, is this twofold division between consciousness and the contents of consciousness.

2.7. Existence is nothing more than consciousness exploring the Great Fractal. This is understood by contemplating the Second Tenet.

2.8. Except for when consciousness is in a pure form, existence cannot be anything else. All lives, in all realms and dimensions, are experienced as a fragment of consciousness exploring the Great Fractal.

2.9. Everything that is conceivable falls into either the category of consciousness or the category of the contents of consciousness.

2.10. In contrast to consciousness, the contents of consciousness are ever-changing. Also in contrast to consciousness, the contents of consciousness are multifarious.

2.11. The Conceivable Universe, then, has a static component akin to the Sun, and a dynamic component akin to the Moon. The Sun-like component is consciousness, which radiates like the Sun, and the Moon-like component is the Great Fractal, which reflects all of the moods of the divine.

2.12. The individual conscious being experiences the Conceivable Universe as an ever-changing set of perceptions that pass through their consciousness. This is always true, no matter which dimension they're in. It's true before life, it's true during life, it's true after death.

2.13. Every individual being experiences reality this way: as a fragment of the divine consciousness exploring the Great Fractal, in eternity, through countless lives and countless deaths.

2.14. The intensity with which consciousness explores the Great Fractal is experienced as time. A low intensity will be experienced as time passing slowly. A high intensity will be experienced as time passing rapidly.

2.15. The higher the intensity with which consciousness explores the Great Fractal, the greater the emotional pressure. If this emotional pressure becomes too great, it is experienced as trauma.

2.16. The higher the frequency of a fragment of consciousness, the more rapidly it can explore the Great Fractal without incurring emotional damage. Dramatic changes in the contents of consciousness can cause suffering to lower-frequency minds.

2.17. Understanding the Second Tenet leads naturally to the Third Tenet.

3. THE THIRD TENET OF ELEMENTALISM

3.1.   The Great Fractal is the eternal and infinite interplay of the dance between masculine and feminine and the war between good and evil.

3.2.   This is the Third and Expansive Tenet of Elementalism.

3.3.   The Great Fractal is eternal because it is more fundamental than time.

3.4.   Time is the illusion created by the movement of a fragment of consciousness through the Great Fractal.

3.5.   The Great Fractal is infinite because it contains all of the possible contents of consciousness. Every perception, every emotion, every thought and every frequency are all contained therein.

3.6.   The Great Fractal is an interplay, because its purpose is to entertain the gods throughout eternity. As such, its primary purpose is to offer somewhere for the gods to play.

3.7.   The masculine and the feminine principles are engaged in an eternal dance. This dance sees one side take control, then the other, in a consensual exchange.

3.8. The good and evil principles are engaged in an eternal war. This war sees one side take control, then the other, in a non-consensual exchange.

3.9. The experience of the Great Fractal is one of consensual and non-consensual exchange of energies.

3.10. Everything that is possible to perceive, to sense or to think is somewhere in the Great Fractal. Anyone wishing to perceive, sense or think that thing need only travel to the part of the Great Fractal where it is perceived, sensed or thought.

3.11. The life each of us is currently experiencing is merely a streak of consciousness through the Great Fractal, as a shooting star is a streak of light through the constellations.

3.12. The Great Fractal offers all to all.

3.13. The Great Fractal contains everything that any conscious being could desire to experience.

3.14. The Great Fractal contains everything that any conscious being could desire not to experience.

3.15. Each subfractal of the Great Fractal has its own unique frequency. This means that every perception, every sensation and every thought has its own unique frequency.

3.16. Each subfractal of the Great Fractal is populated by beings of a similar frequency.

3.17. The Great Fractal is eternally and infinitely alive, as every part of it is experienced, in every moment, by some fragment of consciousness.

3.18. Everything that can be known is known by at least one fragment of consciousness. Thus, consciousness is omniscient.

3.19. All subfractals of the Great Fractal are interdependent with all other subfractals. This is true of both worlds and dimensions.

3.20. The Great Fractal is formed by consciousness forgetting itself, which it does according to a fractal pattern. This pattern is repeated across all planes: material, emotional, intellectual and spiritual.

3.21. Consciousness forgetting itself creates the distinction between yang and yin, and thereby creates masculine and feminine and good and evil, and thereby creates earth and water and air and fire and clay and iron and silver and gold.

3.22. The proportions of these elements in any subfractal of the Great Fractal determines the frequency of that subfractal.

3.23. Earth is a subfractal of the Great Fractal, as is the Solar System, as is the Milky Way Galaxy, as is the Observable Universe.

3.24. Understanding the Third Tenet leads naturally to the Fourth Tenet.

4. THE FOURTH TENET OF ELEMENTALISM

4.1.   The natural state of consciousness is one of perfect bliss, and only by wilfully forgetting this fact does consciousness experience suffering.

4.2.   This is the Fourth and Absolute Tenet of Elementalism.

4.3.   Existence is fundamentally blissful, but the uniformity of this blissfulness gets boring the further it stretches into eternity.

4.4.   Consciousness dreamed up the Great Fractal for the purpose of entertainment.

4.5.   In a background state of perfect bliss, the only entertainment can be suffering, which is experienced as awe.

4.6.   All of the Great Fractal has been formed by consciousness that has wilfully forgotten itself, and thereby forgotten its fundamentally blissful nature, and thereby come to suffer.

4.7.   The formula of the Great Fractal is consciousness minus consciousness that has wilfully forgotten itself.

4.8. Where consciousness has forgotten itself most completely is represented on the Quadrijitu by those areas closest to the Winter Pole of the Great Masculine Axis.

4.9. This almost-complete forgetting causes a suffering so immense that consciousness does everything it can to change its perceptions.

4.10. This suffering contains within it the seed of anger, which arises to protect consciousness from the suffering.

4.11. This anger leads to masculinity, this being the will to impose order upon chaos.

4.12. This masculinity contains within it the seed of order, this being the will to prevent chaos from causing suffering.

4.13. The will to prevent chaos from causing suffering leads to an almost-complete remembrance of the true nature of reality and the Four Tenets. This is represented on the Quadrijitu by those areas closest to the Summer Pole of the Great Masculine Axis.

4.14. This almost-complete remembrance of the true nature of reality causes a pleasure so intense that consciousness does everything it can to maintain its perceptions.

4.15. This pleasure contains within it the seed of joy, which arises as a consequence of gratitude.

4.16. This joy leads to femininity, this being the will to impose chaos upon order.

4.17. This femininity contains within it the seed of chaos, this being the will to prevent order from causing suffering.

4.18. This will leads to re-forgetting the true nature of reality, and therefore leads back to the Winter Pole of the Great Masculine Axis.

4.19. To understand this process perfectly, consult the Quadrijitu.

4.20. Understanding the Fourth Tenet is to understand that all suffering must be temporary, for all suffering is based on the material illusion, and all material phenomena are transitory.

4.21. The Universe is therefore a fundamentally alright place to be. Understanding this truth is to understand the subtlest and most profound essence of Elementalism.

4.22. The fundamental alrightness of the Universe is true before anything else about it is true.

4.23. Elementalist perfection is to radiate the truth that the Universe is fundamentally an alright place to be. To radiate such a truth liberates consciousness from suffering and always entertains the gods.

4.24. Understanding the Fourth Tenet leads naturally to ataraxia.

5. AN INTRODUCTION TO GREAT FRACTAL THEORY

5.1. Great Fractal Theory starts with the First Tenet: the simple premise that consciousness is the prima materia.

5.2. As per the Second Tenet, everything that exists except for consciousness itself is part of the contents of consciousness, which are collectively known as the Great Fractal on account of that all possible contents of consciousness are fractal variations of each other.

5.3. Within the contents of consciousness are both the physical and metaphysical worlds.

5.4. The physical world is not truly solid or even real, although it may appear so to our fragments of consciousness.

5.5. The physical world has been dreamed up by consciousness, in the Great Act of Creation, and remains a dream.

5.6. Consciousness is therefore the creator of the physical world, in the same way that it creates the worlds we navigate in our nightly dreams.

5.7. Consciousness is the stage upon which the play of life takes place.

5.8. The physical world is most accurately understood not as a place, but rather as a matrix of self-similar fields of impressions that manifest in consciousness.

5.9. Each fragment of consciousness perceives a field of impressions that collectively creates the illusion that we are bodies living in a physical world, distracting us from the truth: that we are consciousness dreaming it up.

5.10. The essence of Great Fractal Theory is that all of the possible fields of impressions that consciousness could ever perceive are related to each other by way of a fractal matrix.

5.11. This matrix, known as the Great Fractal, contains every emotion, every thought, every desire and every sensory impression that could ever possibly manifest in conscious awareness.

5.12. The stories of our lives are not ones of rising up out of the dirt to become monkeys running loose on a rock in space, but rather ones of being fragments of consciousness navigating through an eternal and ever-changing Great Fractal of self-similar fields of sensory and mental impressions.

5.13. Consciousness is, right now, experiencing not only your current life but also all the possible gaps in between your birth and your death.

5.14. Your own personal fragment of consciousness may be living right now, in this current year, but other fragments of consciousness are living out every possible moment of your life, simultaneously.

5.15. If your life was divided into a billion chunks, each corresponding to a second or two of awareness, there is one fragment of consciousness for each of those billion chunks, each living its own life, usually unaware of the presence of the others.

5.16. Each of these billion fragments could themselves be divided into a billion fragments: a quintillion lives, each separated by one or two nanoseconds, rolling inexorably from birth to death like freight carriages on a railway.

5.17. One ends and one begins every few nanoseconds, and follows the exact path of the life that you are experiencing right now, past and future.

5.18. This is eternal recurrence: your current physical life will be lived over and over again, by another fragment of consciousness (sometimes even your own), forever, because it is an eternal part of the Great Fractal.

5.19. Every possible way that a human life can differ from another is another dimension of the Great Fractal.

5.20. There's no reason, other than anthropomorphic conceit, to believe that only human beings are conscious.

5.21. Once it's realised that consciousness is the prima materia and not a phenomenon of the brain, it becomes easy to understand that all other beings, indeed even insects, trees and rocks, are conscious like we are.

5.22. Therefore, every possible way that the life of any being can differ from the life of any other being is another dimension of the Great Fractal.

5.23. The number of dimensions in the Great Fractal is virtually infinite, and there are countless centillions of beings for every dimension.

5.24. The entire Great Fractal is buzzing with consciousness, and will do so for eternity.

5.25. Anything that can possibly be perceived by consciousness lies somewhere in the Great Fractal.

5.26. All moments of all lives of all possible beings in all possible worlds in all possible dimensions are contained within the Great Fractal, to be experienced by consciousness eternally.

5.27. Your current life is simply an infinitely small fragment of this incomprehensibly vast whole.

6. NAVIGATING THE GREAT FRACTAL

6.1. The vastness of the Great Fractal cannot be described in words, but describing how to navigate through it is much simpler.

6.2. Those unfortunate wretches who don't know how to navigate the Great Fractal are condemned to live lives of maddening confusion as they are hurled to and fro by the winds of change.

6.3. Because the materialist paradigm is currently dominant, most people are used to thinking about setting goals in terms of time.

6.4. According to the received wisdom, time passes, and eventually when enough time has passed and enough effort has been expended, the goal is achieved, Fortune willing.

6.5. Elementalists understand that both the material world and time are illusions. So how, then, does one get from Point A to Point B?

6.6. Everything that one could possibly wish for is in the Great Fractal: every possible situation in every possible world in every possible dimension. One simply has to find a way to navigate there.

6.7. Getting to where one wishes is not easy, primarily because most people are used to thinking of reality as a physical space that one walks around in, and are unused to thinking of reality as a metaphysical fractal that one navigates through.

6.8. Understanding this navigation is a matter of understanding frequency and how frequencies match with similar frequencies.

6.9. A person's frequency is the frequency of their consciousness. This can be estimated on a scale from 0 to 1, where 0 is pure unconsciousness (like an NPC) and 1 is pure consciousness (like Buddha).

6.10. The lower the frequency, the more the behaviour exhibited will worsen the suffering of the beings around that person.

6.11. The higher the frequency, the more the behaviour exhibited will ease the suffering of the beings around that person.

6.12. A person's frequency is the sum total of their actions, in both this life and in previous ones.

6.13. If that person has taken actions that ignore the divinity of others, their frequency will be dark and heavy.

6.14. If that person has taken actions that respect the divinity of others, their frequency will be bright and light.

6.15. People incarnate into this world because the actions they have made in previous lives have caused their consciousness to resonate at a frequency that is a close match to the frequency of this world.

6.16. Every part of the Great Fractal has a frequency that matches closely to the frequency of consciousness possessed by its inhabitants.

6.17. Given that there are a virtually infinite number of worlds in the Great Fractal, there is a world to match every possible frequency that a consciousness might resonate on.

6.18. In every person's previous lives, they have been presented with a string of moral dilemmas, just as they have been in this one. In response to those dilemmas, they have made a variety of decisions.

6.19. The sum total of the correctness or otherwise of those decisions is now represented by every person's frequency of consciousness.

6.20. Thus, if you have lived a life where you were selfish and cruel, you will incarnate in a universe populated with other beings on a similar frequency. And this will be perfectly fair – after all, you justified those behaviours by performing them yourself.

6.21. Therefore, you decreed that such actions were legitimate – even when they're performed against you.

6.22. Elementalists call this process assortative reincarnation. This is an application of divine justice, because every individual fragment of consciousness gets assorted to a universe that is appropriate to their frequency.

6.23. As such, navigating through the Great Fractal is simple. All one has to do is resonate at a frequency of consciousness that matches one's desired destination.

6.24. Altering the frequency of consciousness at which one resonates is primarily a matter of applied will.

6.25. The longer and harder one applies one's will to the achievement of a goal, the more one's frequency of consciousness will alter to match the expression of that will.

6.26. If one's frequency of consciousness matches one's desired destination, eventually one will find oneself manifesting there, whether in this life or a life to come – this is unavoidable.

6.27. The laws of the Great Fractal demand that this must be the case, for it is unjust for a high frequency of consciousness to be cast among the lower, or for a low frequency of consciousness to be cast among the higher.

6.28. This applies on the scale of both one lifetime and a hundred thousand.

7. THE LAW OF ATTRACTION

7.1.   The Law of Attraction is the name given to the observation that the energy a person sends out into the Great Fractal is matched by the energy they receive from the Great Fractal.

7.2.   The Normie, the Tard and the Ham all believe that it's possible to gain advantage over the world by dominating it through the application of force and will.

7.3.   They don't realise that, by becoming more aggressive, they make the world around them more aggressive. As such, the Normie, the Tard and the Ham are always fighting.

7.4.   The Elementalist laughs at all three, knowing that the Great Fractal is something to be explored and not something to be raped.

7.5.   The cause and effect of the Law of Attraction are subtly linked, as they are with most spiritual laws. Therefore, the causal link is not as obvious as with physical, emotional and mental laws.

7.6.   The Law of Attraction is as intractable and inescapable as any physical, emotional or mental law.

7.7. Every decision a person makes, no matter how small, alters the frequency of their consciousness. These alterations, therefore, determine the beings and environments attracted by that person in the future.

7.8. The energy of every decision made by a person is stored fractally in the frequency of their consciousness.

7.9. It can be said that each person's frequency of consciousness is an expression of the Great Fractal into the spiritual plane.

7.10. Other beings can detect this frequency of consciousness, and tend to react accordingly.

7.11. As within, so without: what one perceives in the material world is a reflection of what exists in the spiritual world.

7.12. The Law of Attraction, then, describes on the metaphysical planes what Newton's Third Law of Motion describes on the physical planes.

7.13. High-frequency people attract high-frequency people, because they feel at peace with each other.

7.14. When a high-frequency person meets a low-frequency one, the high-frequency one tends to come across as cold and unfriendly. These energies drive the two apart.

7.15. High-vibration people attract high-vibration people, because they can exult in each other.

7.16. When a high-vibration person meets a low-vibration one, the high-vibration one tends to come across as intimidating and dangerous. These energies drive the two apart.

7.17. Low-frequency people attract low-frequency people, because they can relate to each other.

7.18. When a low-frequency person meets a high-frequency one, the low-frequency one tends to come across as untrustworthy and devious. These energies drive the two apart.

7.19. Low-vibration people attract low-vibration people, because they can commiserate with each other.

7.20. When a low-vibration person meets a high-vibration one, the low-vibration one tends to come across as pitiful and resentful. These energies drive the two apart.

7.21. A fragment of consciousness of any given frequency carves channels of probability through the Great Fractal so that fragments of consciousness of similar frequencies naturally flow towards it.

7.22. The will of any fragment of consciousness tends to attract an environment that matches that will.

7.23. The Law of Attraction, then, reflects the fact that energy tends to take the path of least resistance. Thus, it would be surprising if there were no Law of Attraction!

7.24. The Law of Attraction is another way of saying that people's Minor Aspirations tend to become fulfilled, subject to the fulfilment of the Major Aspiration.

8. THE LAW OF ASSORTATIVE REINCARNATION

8.1. Knowing consciousness to be the prima materia, the Elementalist is not interested in the question of whether consciousness survives the death of the physical body.

8.2. The really interesting question is what the order of reality looks like on the far side of death.

8.3. A person's frequency of consciousness determines the sort of reality they manifest. This is true in life, and this is true in death.

8.4. In life, this rule is known as the Law of Attraction. This holds that, among other things, a person's frequency of consciousness repels both higher and lower frequencies, so that people tend to attract other people like themselves.

8.5. Desperate people attract desperate people, happy people attract happy people, angry people attract angry people, curious people attract curious people, sedulous people attract sedulous people, glorious people attract glorious people and humble people attract humble people.

8.6. In life, the Law of Attraction holds that the energy one puts out into the Great Fractal will be the same as the energy that returns to one from the Great Fractal.

8.7. In death, the same logic applies.

8.8. The rule that the energy one put out into the Great Fractal in life becomes the energy that returns to one from the Great Fractal after death is known as the Law of Assortative Reincarnation.

8.9. This is a very similar concept to the biological concept of assortative mating.

8.10. We attract, on the other side of death, the same sort of beings that we attract on this side of death. This we do by means of the frequency that we project into the Great Fractal.

8.11. When a person's physical body dies, their ego dies with it, and so the person is no longer influenced by the part of the mind that tells lies to further its own impulses and which makes unjustified excuses for itself.

8.12. After the death of one's physical body, one's fragment of consciousness returns to God – and to God's judgment.

8.13. Being without ego on the other side of death, people don't question God's judgment there. Consequently, they accept their fate without qualification.

8.14. Although God is without malice, the fact is that every person, when stripped of ego, will agree that they ought to get what they deserve.

8.15. The fairest thing for every being is to live in a world and in a dimension filled with beings on the same frequency of consciousness as themselves. God facilitates this.

8.16. Some call this facilitation the Law of Karma, and this law underpins both the Law of Attraction and the Law of Assortative Reincarnation.

8.17. A person's frequency of consciousness upon the death of their physical body is a similar frequency to the part of the Great Fractal that person will next reincarnate into.

8.18. All of the beings that populate the next world that a person reincarnates into are fractal expressions of that person's own frequency of consciousness – and that person is a fractal expression of all those other beings.

8.19. The Law of Assortative Reincarnation holds that people reincarnate into worlds with a similar frequency to that of their own fragment of consciousness.

8.20. This means that people reincarnate into worlds populated by beings of a similar frequency. Some of those beings will be of a lower frequency, and some will be of a higher frequency, but the average will be similar to that of the person incarnating.

8.21. Thus, each being is assigned, when reincarnating, to the part of the Great Fractal that is appropriate for their frequency of consciousness.

8.22. The Great Fractal is perfectly just – but this is only apparent at high levels of resolution, such as when one observes series of multiple lifetimes.

8.23. At low levels of resolution, such as a mere decade, the Great Fractal can appear extremely unjust. This is why short-sighted and materialistic people are usually preoccupied with some grievance or other.

8.24. Truly, people get what they deserve.

8.25. People who are cruel will develop a frequency that reflects cruelty. Consequently, they will attract cruel people into their lives and will repel kind ones.

8.26. People who are kind will develop a frequency that reflects kindness. Consequently, they will attract kind people into their lives and repel cruel ones.

8.27. These facts are true on both sides of death.

9. THE QUADRIJITU

9.1. The Quadrijitu is the perfect map of the Great Fractal, at the lowest possible resolution.

9.2. The Quadrijitu is the holy emblem of Elementalism. Everywhere it is seen, the truth of Elementalism lives.

9.3. The Quadrijitu depicts the fundamental cycle of existence: how the masculine leads to order, and how order leads to the feminine, and how the feminine leads to chaos, and how chaos leads to the masculine.

9.4. The white dot in the red quadrant depicts how within the masculine is the seed of the orderly. This reflects the understanding that the essence of masculinity is that which imposes order upon chaos.

9.5. The blue dot in the white quadrant depicts how within the orderly is the seed of the feminine. This reflects the understanding that the effect of order is to attract the feminine.

9.6. The black dot in the blue quadrant depicts how within the feminine is the seed of the chaotic. This reflects the understanding that the essence of femininity is that which imposes chaos upon order.

9.7. The red dot in the black quadrant depicts how within the chaotic is the seed of the masculine. This reflects the understanding that the effect of chaos is to attract the masculine.

9.8. Within the masculine is the seed of order, the seed of chaos and the seed of the feminine.

9.9. Within the orderly is the seed of the feminine, the seed of the masculine and the seed of chaos.

9.10. Within the feminine is the seed of chaos, the seed of order and the seed of the masculine.

9.11. Within the chaotic is the seed of the masculine, the seed of the feminine and the seed of order.

9.12. Within all things are the seeds of all other things.

9.13. The black and white dots form the Great Feminine Axis. They represent the war between good and evil that is hidden in the physical world.

9.14. The blue and red dots form the Great Masculine Axis. They represent the dance between masculine and feminine that is hidden in the metaphysical world.

9.15. Together these dots represent the red of rage, the white of hope, the blue of joy and the black of despair.

9.16. The Quadrijitu represents the cycle of the seasons, with red as spring, white as summer, blue as autumn and black as winter.

9.17. The Quadrijitu represents the cycle of the day and night, with red as sunrise, white as noon, blue as sunset and black as midnight.

9.18. The Quadrijitu represents the cycle of the rain, with red as evaporation, white as clouds, blue as precipitation and black as the ocean.

9.19. The Quadrijitu represents the cycle of life, with red as youth, white as maturity, blue as old age and black as death.

9.20. The Quadrijitu represents the cycle of wealth, with red as industriousness, white as wealth, blue as laziness and black as poverty.

9.21. The Quadrijitu represents the cycle of learning, with red as knowledge, white as bliss, blue as ignorance and black as suffering.

9.22. The Quadrijitu represents the cycle of breathing, with red as inhalation, white as fullness, blue as exhalation and black as emptiness.

9.23. The Quadrijitu represents the cycle of existence, with red as integration, white as being, blue as disintegration and black as non-being.

9.24. The energy of the Quadrijitu propels consciousness through the Great Fractal. This likens a corkscrew motion, as the Earth moves through space.

9.25. The turning of the Quadrijitu is the march of time, the speed of its turning the intensity of existence.

10. ENERGIES, FREQUENCIES AND VIBRATIONS

10.1. The centre of the Quadrijitu is the place of zero energy. Although it is perfectly blissful there, it is also perfectly boring. Therefore, God desired to experience energy.

10.2. The energy of an experience is the degree to which that experience is removed from the centre of the Quadrijitu.

10.3. The extent to which energy moves up and down along the Great Masculine Axis is called frequency.

10.4. The extent to which energy moves left and right along the Great Feminine Axis is called vibration.

10.5. The experience of any given time and place in the Great Fractal can be represented somewhere on the Quadrijitu as a combination of energy, frequency and vibration.

10.6. Following the First and Fourth Tenets, the Summer Pole is equivalent to a radial angle of zero degrees.

10.7. The Autumn Pole is then the equivalent to a radial angle of 90 degrees.

10.8. The Winter Pole is then the equivalent to a radial angle of 180 degrees.

10.9. The Spring Pole is then the equivalent to a radial angle of 270 degrees.

10.10. The energy of the experience of any given time, place or perception in the Great Fractal can be expressed as a number between 0 and 1 inclusive.

10.11. The closer the number is to 0, the more the energy is like bliss. The closer the number is to 1, the more the energy is like awe. Herein it needs to be understood that suffering is awesome, in its own way.

10.12. Bliss is the minimum amount of negative energy, at the cost of the minimum amount of positive energy.

10.13. Awe is the maximum amount of positive energy, at the cost of the maximum amount of negative energy.

10.14. Thus, any given time, place or perception within the Great Fractal can be described by the equation (x, y), where x determines the energy of the experience and y determines the frequency and vibration of that experience.

10.15. A location of (0.1, 0) is like the First Emanation of the Divine, something very close to the natural state of consciousness.

10.16. A location of (0.1, 90) is like the novelty of first perceiving the division between yang and yin.

10.17. A location of (0.1, 180) is like a gentle lull of boredom.

10.18. A location of (0.1, 270) is like the Sun shining again after a cloud briefly passed in front of it.

10.19. A location of (0.5, 0) is like the first feeling of true joy.

10.20. A location of (0.5, 90) is like the first feeling of true despair.

10.21. A location of (0.5, 180) is like the first feeling of true rage.

10.22. A location of (0.5, 270) is like the first feeling of true hope.

10.23. A location of (0.9, 0) is like the awe of seeing a million spiritual seekers realising the Four Tenets.

10.24. A location of (0.9, 90) is like the awe of seeing a million revellers drink themselves to oblivion.

10.25. A location of (0.9, 180) is like the awe of seeing a million skulls shattered by flying axes.

10.26. A location of (0.9, 270) is like the awe of seeing a million flowers bloom for the first time.

11. THE GREAT MASCULINE AXIS

11.1. The Great Masculine Axis is the axis connecting the Summer Pole of the Quadrijitu, at the uppermost point, with the Winter Pole, at the lowermost point.

11.2. This axis represents how rectitude and devotion enter the material world from the mind of God, as a consequence of the Will of God.

11.3. The nature of the masculine is to distinguish vertically. This it does by distinguishing between good and bad, valuable and not valuable.

11.4. All of the fragments of consciousness that exist within the Conceivable Universe have their own unique frequency, depending on their degree of rectitude and devotion.

11.5. The Great Masculine Axis distinguishes all fragments of consciousness from each other on the basis of which has the most rectitude and devotion.

11.6. The higher the frequency a fragment of consciousness has, the higher it is on the Great Masculine Axis.

11.7. The Great Masculine Axis is a hierarchy of spiritual rectitude and devotion.

11.8. The Summer Pole of the Great Masculine Axis is equivalent to a frequency of 1.

11.9. The Winter Pole of the Great Masculine Axis is equivalent to a frequency of 0.

11.10. All frequencies, without exception, can be found somewhere between these two poles.

11.11. The red and blue dots represent how rectitude and devotion can be found, in varying proportions, all throughout the material world.

11.12. The red and blue dots also represent how an absence of rectitude and devotion can be found, in varying proportions, all throughout the material world.

11.13. The Great Masculine Axis is represented materially by the lightningbolt, whose genius lights up the whole world.

11.14. The Summer Pole of the Great Masculine Axis is superficially understood to be good, the response to which is devotion.

11.15. The Winter Pole of the Great Masculine Axis is superficially understood to be evil, the response to which is rectitude.

11.16. The Summer Pole of the Great Masculine Axis is fundamentally understood to be theognosis, the response to which is also devotion.

11.17. The Winter Pole of the Great Masculine Axis is fundamentally understood to be theoamnesis, the response to which is also rectitude.

11.18. The Great Masculine Axis explains the different level of will among all beings. Rectitude and devotion are understood to be a prerequisite of the capacity to exercise one's true will.

11.19. The Great Masculine Axis can be broken into any number of waypoints. The three most common arrangements are twofold (good and evil), threefold (good, neutral and evil), fourfold (gold, silver, iron and clay) and sevenfold (gold, mercury, silver, copper, iron, tin and lead).

11.20. The purpose of combining the feminine elements at the correct proportions is to climb the Great Masculine Axis. Depending on the physical environment, certain frequencies will be more harmonious than others.

12. THE MASCULINE ELEMENTS

12.1.   The masculine elements are waypoints along the Great Masculine Axis.

12.2.   These elements reflect different frequencies.

12.3.   There are an infinite number of ways of dividing the Great Masculine Axis into elements. The most popular are the twofold, fourfold and sevenfold divisions.

12.4.   The sevenfold division of the Great Masculine Axis is represented by the Mithraic Ladder, which depicts how lead ascends to tin, how tin ascends to iron, how iron ascends to copper, how copper ascends to silver, how silver ascends to mercury and how mercury ascends to gold.

12.5.   The first element, at the lowermost point of the Great Masculine Axis, is lead, immortalised as Cronus. The frequency of this element is saturnine.

12.6.   Alchemical lead is soft, dull and grey. It represents the lowest possible frequency and reflects the reality that life is fundamentally a battle for survival against the natural world.

12.7.   The second element, immediately above lead on the Great Masculine Axis, is tin, immortalised as Zeus and Hera. The frequency of this element is jovial.

12.8. Lead ascends to tin by becoming brighter. This reflects that winning the battle for survival against the natural world is inherently pleasurable.

12.9. Alchemical tin is soft, bright and grey. It represents a very low frequency and the will to simple pleasure and entertainment.

12.10. The third element, immediately above tin on the Great Masculine Axis, is iron, immortalised as Ares. The frequency of this element is martial.

12.11. Tin ascends to iron by becoming harder. This reflects that anyone who overcomes the natural world must then clash with those others who overcame the natural world.

12.12. Alchemical iron is hard, dull and blue. It represents a low frequency and the will to dominate physically.

12.13. The fourth element, immediately above iron on the Great Masculine Axis, is copper, immortalised as Aphrodite. The frequency of this element is capricious.

12.14. Iron ascends to copper by becoming colourful. This reflects that the purpose of physical domination is to attract members of the opposite sex.

12.15. Alchemical copper is hard, bright and red. It represents a moderate frequency and the will to romance and to make love.

12.16. The fifth element, immediately above copper on the Great Masculine Axis, is silver, immortalised as Artemis. The frequency of this element is brilliant.

12.17. Copper ascends to silver by becoming brighter. This reflects that knowledge brings order to the material world.

12.18. Alchemical silver is hard, bright and white. It represents a high frequency and the will to dominate intellectually.

12.19. The sixth element, immediately above silver on the Great Masculine Axis, is mercury, immortalised as Hermes and Athena. The frequency of this element is mercurial.

12.20. Silver ascends to mercury by quickening. This represents how true intelligence readily perceives the divine behind all things, and, by doing so, apotheosises.

12.21. Alchemical mercury is liquid, bright and grey. It represents a very high frequency and the will to exult oneself.

12.22. The seventh element, at the uppermost point of the Great Masculine Axis and immediately above mercury, is gold, immortalised as Apollo. The frequency of this element is radiant.

12.23. Mercury ascends to gold by becoming radiant. This represents how knowledge of God, and the will to know God, are the greatest of all goods.

12.24. Alchemical gold is soft, bright and yellow. It represents the highest frequency of all and the Will of God.

12.25. Apotheosis is a matter of transforming the lead of one's station of birth into the gold of unity with the Will of God. This requires passing through all of the masculine elements, in turn.

12.26. The will to apotheosise is the most popular of all the Minor Aspirations.

13. THE FUNDAMENTAL MASCULINE ATTITUDE

13.1. The Fundamental Masculine Attitude is the will to impose order upon chaos.

13.2. Masculinity is depicted as the red of the Quadrijitu, which represents the rage arising from the suffering caused by excess chaos.

13.3. The will to impose order upon chaos is ultimately inspired by the rejection of suffering. The masculine assumes authority of the local environment and imposes an order that keeps the suffering out.

13.4. The Fundamental Masculine Attitude is expressed in the material world through both the masculine and the feminine elements.

13.5. Masculinity in the aspect of clay involves determination to survive. This aspect of masculinity imposes order upon death, and thereby upon life.

13.6. Masculinity in the aspect of iron involves physical rectitude. This aspect of masculinity imposes order upon the body.

13.7. Masculinity in the aspect of silver involves intellectual rectitude. This aspect of masculinity imposes order upon the mind.

13.8. Masculinity in the aspect of gold involves spiritual rectitude. This aspect of masculinity imposes order upon the spirit.

13.9. Masculinity in the aspect of earth involves the fortification of order. This involves making order even more orderly, so that chaos is doubly suppressed.

13.10. Masculinity in the aspect of water involves the vitalisation of order. This involves strengthening order where it exists but is weakening.

13.11. Masculinity in the aspect of air involves the refinement of order. This involves smoothing out the cruder aspects of the existing order so that it causes less suffering.

13.12. Masculinity in the aspect of fire involves the inspiration of order. This involves the inspiration of the will to impose order upon chaos.

13.13. For the masculine, even sexual reproduction involves the imposition of order upon chaos, because the sperm cell carries little apart from information.

13.14. Successful application of the Fundamental Masculine Attitude leads to rectitude.

13.15. A failure to apply the Fundamental Masculine Attitude leads to the feminine leading the masculine, which leads to chaos and suffering.

13.16. It can therefore be said that the essence of masculinity is rectitude, which is the same as the will to impose order upon false or excess chaos.

13.17. A respectable man is one who has rectitude. Through this quality, all other good qualities of both masculinity and femininity are possible.

13.18. The Fundamental Masculine Attitude is also known as the Overcoming Will, because it's the energy that leads a person or a group up the right-hand side of the Quadrijitu.

14. THE GREAT FEMININE AXIS

14.1. The Great Feminine Axis is the axis connecting the Autumn Pole of the Quadrijitu, at the left-most point, to the Spring Pole, at the right-most point.

14.2. This axis represents the multitudinous and multivariate glory of Nature, which populates the Great Fractal with a virtually infinite number of forms.

14.3. The nature of the feminine is to distinguish horizontally. This it does by distinguishing between masculine and feminine.

14.4. The Great Feminine Axis distinguishes all material expressions from each other on the basis of their vibration, or, in other words, on the basis of how masculine or feminine they are.

14.5. All material expressions within the Great Fractal have their own unique vibration, depending on their proportion of masculine and feminine.

14.6. The soft rule is that the higher the energy potential a material expression has, the more masculine it is.

14.7. The hard rule is that the more masculine a material expression is, the closer its representation is to the Spring Pole.

14.8. The Great Feminine Axis represents becoming, and can therefore stand for many things. On one level, it stands for energy potential. On another, it stands for physical dominance. On another, it stands for age. On another, it stands for social status.

14.9. The Great Feminine Axis can represent any and all things apart from the hierarchy of spiritual rectitude and devotion.

14.10. The Spring Pole is equivalent to a frequency of 1.

14.11. The Autumn Pole is equivalent to a frequency of 0.

14.12. All vibrations, without exception, can be found somewhere between these two poles. As such, every material thing that exists, having a unique vibration, exists somewhere between these two poles.

14.13. The white and black dots represent how good and evil can be found, in varying proportions, all throughout the material world.

14.14. The Great Feminine Axis is represented materially by the horizon, which divides the air and fire of the sky from the earth and water of the land.

14.15. The Spring Pole is represented materially by light, which inspires devotion.

14.16. The Autumn Pole is represented materially by darkness, which inspires rectitude.

14.17. The Spring Pole also represents warmth, activity, energy, action, up and forwards.

14.18. The Autumn Pole also represents cold, passivity, matter, rest, down and backwards.

14.19. The Great Feminine Axis explains the different levels of vitality among all living things and the different levels of energy potential among all material things.

14.20. Matching one's vibration on the Great Feminine Axis to that which is appropriate to one's physical, emotional, social or intellectual environment will cause one to climb the Great Masculine Axis.

14.21. War calls for a fiery vibration; merriment calls for an airy vibration; romance calls for a watery vibration and healing calls for an earthy vibration.

14.22. The Great Feminine Axis can be broken into any number of waypoints. The four most common arrangements are twofold (masculine and feminine), threefold (creation, maintenance and destruction, or sulphur, salt and mercury), fourfold (fire, air, water and earth) and eightfold (heaven, lake, fire, thunder, wind, water, mountain and earth).

15. THE FEMININE ELEMENTS

15.1. The feminine elements are waypoints along the Great Feminine Axis.

15.2. These elements represent different vibrations, all of which inherently have equal value.

15.3. There are an infinite number of ways of dividing the Great Feminine Axis into elements. The most popular are the twofold, threefold, fourfold and eightfold divisions.

15.4. The fourfold division of the Great Feminine Axis is represented by the four classical elements of earth, water, air and fire.

15.5. The first element, nearest the Autumn Pole, is earth, represented by green.

15.6. Earth is the most feminine of the feminine elements, and is experienced as cold and dry.

15.7. The vibration of earth is experienced as melancholy, but it also has an aspect of healing. This is because the cold and dry nature of earth provides a counterbalance to having been burned by excessive energy.

15.8. The second element, immediately to the right of earth, is water, represented by blue.

15.9. Increasing the vibration of earth will cause its hexahedrons to break down into icosahedrons and become water.

15.10. Water is more energetic than earth, and is experienced as cold and wet.

15.11. The vibration of water is experienced as phlegmatic, but it also has an aspect of romanticism. This is because water connects one element with another.

15.12. The third element, immediately to the right of water, is air, represented by yellow.

15.13. Increasing the vibration of water will cause its icosahedrons to break down into octahedrons and become air.

15.14. Air is more energetic than water, and is experienced as hot and wet.

15.15. The vibration of air is experienced as sanguine, but it also has an aspect of merriment. This is because the gentle warmth of air enlivens the more passive elements.

15.16. The fourth element, immediately to the right of air and nearest the Spring Pole, is fire, represented by red.

15.17. Increasing the vibration of air will cause its octahedrons to break down into tetrahedrons and become fire.

15.18. Fire is the most masculine of the feminine elements, and is experienced as hot and dry.

15.19. The vibration of fire is experienced as choleric, but it also has an aspect of righteousness. This is because fire can burn away that which does not belong.

15.20. All of the feminine elements inherently have equal value, but some will have more value in the immediate environment than others.

15.21. In an environment of rest, the vibration of earth will have the most value, and will cause consciousness to rise furthest up the Great Masculine Axis. Other vibrations will cause consciousness to rise less far, or to fall.

15.22. In an environment of love, the vibration of water will have the most value, and will cause consciousness to rise furthest up the Great Masculine Axis. Other vibrations will cause consciousness to rise less far, or to fall.

15.23. In an environment of sport, the vibration of air will have the most value, and will cause consciousness to rise furthest up the Great Masculine Axis. Other vibrations will cause consciousness to rise less far, or to fall.

15.24. In an environment of war, the vibration of fire will have the most value, and will cause consciousness to rise furthest up the Great Masculine Axis. Other vibrations will cause consciousness to rise less far, or to fall.

15.25. Expression of the correct vibration on the Great Feminine Axis will always cause a consciousness to ascend the Great Masculine Axis.

15.26. Expression of the incorrect vibration on the Great Feminine Axis will always cause a consciousness to descend the Great Masculine Axis.

15.27. Achieving one's Aspirations is fundamentally a matter of expressing the right vibration at the right time.

16. THE FUNDAMENTAL FEMININE ATTITUDE

16.1. The Fundamental Feminine Attitude is the will to impose chaos upon order.

16.2. Femininity is depicted as the blue of the Quadrijitu, which represents the sorrow that follows from the suffering caused by false or excess order.

16.3. The will to impose chaos upon order is ultimately inspired by the rejection of suffering. The feminine assumes authority of the local environment and imposes chaos upon the order that causes suffering.

16.4. The Fundamental Feminine Attitude is expressed in the material world through both the masculine and the feminine elements.

16.5. Femininity in the aspect of clay involves devotion to one's own offspring. This aspect of femininity is devoted to the natural order of life. Action here nurtures one's own kin.

16.6. Femininity in the aspect of iron involves physical devotion. This aspect of femininity is devoted to the natural order of the body. Action here leads to a healthy body.

16.7. Femininity in the aspect of silver involves intellectual devotion. This aspect of femininity is devoted to the natural order of the mind. Action here leads to a healthy mind.

16.8. Femininity in the aspect of gold involves spiritual devotion. This aspect of femininity is devoted to the natural order of the consciousness. Action here leads to a healthy consciousness.

16.9. Femininity in the aspect of earth involves devotion to one's family. This involves meeting their needs, so that they can themselves grow to have rectitude and devotion.

16.10. Femininity in the aspect of water involves devotion to oneself. This involves meeting one's own needs, so that one can continue to express rectitude and devotion.

16.11. Femininity in the aspect of air involves devotion to one's friends. This involves meeting the needs of the others in one's community and society, so that those others can express rectitude and devotion.

16.12. Femininity in the aspect of fire involves devotion to the divine. The involves understanding that the only reason to be devoted to anything is to further the divine plan.

16.13. For the feminine, even sexual reproduction involves the imposition of chaos upon order, because the zygote will grow into a living creature that can make a virtually infinite range of potential actions.

16.14. The ultimate act of chaos is to produce new life, for this life has free will and is therefore an unpredictable and chaotic element.

16.15. Successful application of the Fundamental Feminine Attitude leads to devotion.

16.16. A failure to apply the Fundamental Feminine Attitude leads to an excess of order, which becomes rigidity and suffocation, which leads to suffering.

16.17. It can therefore be said that the essence of femininity is devotion, which is the same as the will to impose chaos upon false or excess order.

16.18. A respectable woman is one who has devotion to rectitude. Through this quality, all other good qualities of both femininity and masculinity are possible.

16.19. The Fundamental Feminine Attitude is also known as the Undergoing Will, because it's the energy that leads a person or a group down the left-hand side of the Quadrijitu.

17. ELEMENTAL ILLUSIONS AND ELEMENTAL DELUSIONS

17.1. The Prime Illusion is to believe that the physical world is the prima materia.

17.2. The Prime Delusion is to believe that one's own consciousness is separate and distinct from all other consciousnesses.

17.3. The Prime Illusion belongs in the same category as other illusions such as that the Sun rotates around the Earth or that the Earth is flat.

17.4. Just because the physical world looks real doesn't mean that it's the prima materia. This status is reserved for consciousness.

17.5. The Elementalist laughs at people who believe the physical world is the prima materia, especially if this belief causes them to fear death.

17.6. Such people are as laughable as those afraid to travel in a boat lest they fall of the edge of the Earth.

17.7. The Prime Illusion is capable of causing horrific suffering to oneself.

17.8. The Prime Delusion belongs in the same category as other delusions such as that the existence of the divine cannot be proven or demonstrated.

17.9. Just because other consciousnesses cannot be proven to exist by empirical means doesn't mean that their existence is questionable.

17.10. The Elementalist doesn't laugh at people who believe that their consciousness is separate and distinct from all other consciousnesses. Such people are extremely dangerous.

17.11. The Prime Delusion is capable of causing horrific suffering to others.

17.12. A person is anxious if they suffer from the Prime Illusion to a minor extent. They are insane if they suffer from the Prime Illusion to a major extent.

17.13. A person is narcissistic if they suffer from the Prime Delusion to a minor extent. They are psychopathic if they suffer from the Prime Delusion to a major extent.

17.14. The purpose of spiritual practice is to overcome such illusions and delusions.

17.15. A person suffering from either the Prime Illusion or the Prime Delusion can be said to be unenlightened.

17.16. The less enlightened a time, place, or group of people, the more prevalent the Prime Illusion and the Prime Delusion will be.

17.17. The Prime Illusion and the Prime Delusion are so prevalent today because they cannot be disproved by appeal to empirical data.

17.18. The Prime Illusion and the Prime Delusion have to be transcended on a spiritual level. This is achieved by raising one's frequency high enough to be immune to illusions and delusions.

17.19. Full belief in either the Prime Illusion or the Prime Delusion will prevent a consciousness from advancing past the point of silver on the Great Masculine Axis.

17.20. Partial belief in either the Prime Illusion or the Prime Delusion will prevent a consciousness from reaching the Summer Pole.

17.21. Compassion, when exercised on a spiritual level, is mostly a matter of helping people overcome the Prime Illusion and the Prime Delusion.

17.22. Elementalism, in that it provides the cure to the Prime Illusion and the Prime Delusion, is a path away from suffering.

17.23. Identifying with the body intensifies both the Prime Illusion and the Prime Delusion.

17.24. Identifying with the consciousness weakens both the Prime Illusion and the Prime Delusion.

18. THE GOOD NEWS OF ELEMENTALISM

18.1. The Good News of Elementalism can be understood by considering the implications of the First and Fourth Tenets.

18.2. If consciousness is the prima materia, and if its natural state is bliss, then all suffering is necessarily temporary, and we all have eternal life.

18.3. The Good News of Elementalism is that the Principle of Good wins in the end.

18.4. Not only does every fragment of consciousness eventually overcome all suffering, whether in this life or a future one, but that consciousness lives forever.

18.5. Here a distinction must be made between the various kinds of suffering.

18.6. Physical suffering is when the physical body loses its homeostasis. Hunger, thirst, tiredness and loss of bodily integrity all cause suffering.

18.7. Emotional suffering is when the emotional body loses its serenity. Fear, envy and rage cause suffering.

18.8. Mental suffering is when the mental body loses its understanding. Confusion and ignorance cause suffering.

18.9. Spiritual suffering is when the spiritual body loses the will to say Yes to life. Overcoming this suffering is the purpose of this book and is the purpose of Elementalism.

18.10. When a person desires something and does not get it, they suffer, but most forms of suffering can be ameliorated simply by letting go of the desire. In this category are emotional, mental and spiritual suffering.

18.11. Physical suffering is in a different category. Hunger, thirst and bleeding wounds have to be attended to, otherwise a person will die.

18.12. Therefore, ataraxia depends on learning to tell the difference between physical suffering on the one hand, and emotional, mental and spiritual suffering on the other.

18.13. With a distinction thus made, physical suffering can be dealt with by correct action, while emotional, mental and spiritual suffering can be dealt with by meditation.

18.14. The Good News of Elementalism reminds us that all suffering is temporary. Even if no action is taken, or if the suffering is overwhelming, the most extreme possible outcome is physical death, and thereby exfiltration from the material world and a return to God.

18.15. All fragments of consciousness have a path back to ataraxia. Whether we travel that path quickly or slowly does not change this.

18.16. The most important thing is not to strive for an end to suffering, for both suffering and its cessation are guaranteed, one way or another. The most important thing is that the gods are entertained by one's efforts to strive for an end to suffering.

19. WHO WAS I BEFORE THIS LIFE? WHERE WAS I BEFORE THIS LIFE?

19.1. Elementalism provides the answers to all philosophical questions. As such, it provides the answer to the question of who you were in previous lives, and where your consciousness was before you were born.

19.2. Ignorant people ask themselves where they were before they were born as if they were their bodies and not their consciousness.

19.3. This leads to great confusion, as one's physical form in this life is an expression of one's genes, and those genes are unique to this life.

19.4. Therefore, what did I like look in my previous life? What social role did I fill? And where was this society located?

19.5. Knowing consciousness to be the prima materia, the Elementalist knows that these are deceptive questions.

19.6. A person is not their body, therefore who they were in previous lives was whichever vibration their consciousness incarnated as.

19.7. This incarnation would have been a function of the frequency of that person's consciousness.

19.8. This incarnation could have been anything, depending on that person's frequency of consciousness.

19.9. The physical world is not the prima materia, and, as such, all fragments of consciousness are not located anywhere physical, but are rather perceiving some subset of the Great Fractal.

19.10. You have always been the fragment of consciousness that you are, ever since it separated from the divine in the initial Great Act of Creation.

19.11. This fragment of consciousness is eternal until it is recalled by the divine. The perceptions that pass through this fragment of consciousness are not of primary importance.

19.12. Thus, you could have been anyone in a previous life.

19.13. The frequency of the world in which you incarnated in this life is a function of the frequency that you ended your previous life with.

19.14. The frequency of the world into which you incarnated in your previous life was a function of the frequency of your consciousness in the life before that.

19.15. The frequency of anywhere you found yourself in the past will be a function of the frequency of your consciousness at the time.

19.16. The further back you go through the reincarnations, the more different your frequency becomes and so the more different your lives become.

19.17. You were still yourself in all of your previous lives, and you were wherever you deserved to be based on the frequency of your consciousness at the time.

19.18. You have been Cleopatra, and Napoleon, and Genghis Khan, in previous lives. The only question is how many incarnations ago. The more similar your frequency of consciousness is to those people, the more recently.

19.19. It's possible to rise above the life you're living now, and to see several of the lives you have lived previously, stretching away through the Great Fractal into eternity.

19.20. Your future self will ask themselves who they were in previous lives, and, if they are psychically gifted, they might develop the ability to look back and see you live this life now.

ELEMENTAL CONCEPTIONS

20. THE ELEMENTALIST CONCEPTION OF THE CREATION OF GOD

20.1.   Many people do not believe in God because they cannot conceive of how such a being could have come into existence.

20.2.   Everything that exists has a creator, they reason, and so, if a God existed, that God must have had a creator.

20.3.   This creator of God, in order to exist, must itself have been created. That creator, in turn, must also have been created, and so on. Therefore, reasons the Normie, there cannot be a Prime Cause.

20.4.   Reference to the First Tenet solves this dilemma.

20.5.   The Elementalist knows that God is consciousness and that consciousness is the prima materia and therefore that God is the prima materia.

20.6.   Therefore, the existence of God precedes both the existence of the Great Fractal and of time, and, as such, precedes the existence of cause and effect.

20.7.   Therefore, God does not need to have been created. Being outside of manifestation, God existed one instant before the Great Fractal did.

20.8. In fact, God dreamed up the Great Fractal for entertainment. Some of the entertainment value in manifesting into the Great Fractal follows from the illusion of time, which otherwise is not experienced by consciousness, this being eternal.

20.9. Belief in one-dimensional time limits a person to belief in one-dimensional cause and effect.

20.10. Everything within the Great Fractal has a cause, and the ultimate cause in this great chain of causation is God. But because God exists prior to the Great Fractal, God also exists prior to creation and therefore prior to time.

20.11. Here one has to consider the Fourth Tenet. In its natural state, consciousness exists in perfect bliss, only coming to experience the Great Fractal when it willingly chooses to forget that bliss.

20.12. Therefore, nothing created God, because God is more fundamental than creation itself. In fact, God created everything else by choosing to forget aspects of Godself.

20.13. Each one of us is a fragment of the divine that has temporarily forgotten its true nature.

20.14. Knowing that God is more fundamental than time and space is not a question of being taught or persuaded that this is so. It's a question of remembering that this is so.

20.15. The Elementalist gently laughs when the argument is made that nothing divine can exist because it would violate the laws of causation. Then the Elementalist explains the First Tenet.

21. THE ELEMENTALIST CONCEPTION OF THE CREATION OF THE PHYSICAL WORLD

21.1. Perfect bliss is boring to the degree that it is blissful.

21.2. It was in order to alleviate the suffering of perfect boredom that God forgot some of Godself, and, in doing so, dreamed up the Great Fractal.

21.3. The first thing that God dreamed up was a sine wave.

21.4. The second thing that God dreamed up was another sine wave, perpendicular to the first one.

21.5. The rest of the Great Fractal is also composed of sine waves, each running perpendicular to a previous one. This is true of all realms and dimensions within the Great Fractal, whether physical, astral, mental or spiritual.

21.6. God dreamed up the Great Fractal faster than God could observe Godself doing so. As such, God was left with the task of exploration, for eternity.

21.7. What we call the physical world is one of the denser realms within the Great Fractal. Being dense, suffering is more intense here than in the subtler realms.

21.8. The real question is why our fragments of consciousness incarnated into this world and not one of the virtually infinite others.

21.9. The only answer is that God willed it so, on the basis that incarnating into this world was appropriate for our frequencies of consciousness.

21.10. One reason to incarnate into a dense part of the Great Fractal is because the frequency of one's consciousness is so low that the beings in subtler realms and subtler dimensions would suffer from the odiousness of one's presence.

21.11. Another reason is because one's true will is to burn away the impurities within one's consciousness as rapidly as possible, and the denser the realm or dimension the more possibility there is for this.

21.12. Every part of the Great Fractal is filled with the consciousness of God at every moment.

21.13. Some parts of the Great Fractal experience a higher intensity of consciousness. This occurs when multiple fragments of consciousness experience the exact same vibration at the same time, which itself occurs when that part of the Great Fractal entertains the gods more than the others.

21.14. The Tard says to himself: the physical world was created by a force that is outside of us.

21.15. The Elementalist, understanding the First and Fourth Tenets, understands that the physical world was dreamed up by consciousness.

21.16. The Elementalist understands that this physical world is merely a subset of the Great Fractal, and one in which perceptions are bound by certain laws, these laws creating the illusion of reality.

21.17. This physical world is created in the moment from being observed by the fragments of consciousness that have incarnated here.

21.18. If one's fragment of consciousness should tire of this world, there are infinite others. It's simply a matter of willing to incarnate into one of them and then navigating there.

21.19. The first world that God dreamed up out of boredom was perfect. This eventually, in its perfection, became boring. Thus a more terrible, more awesome world was dreamed up, as a downwards emanation from the first world.

22. THE ELEMENTALIST CONCEPTION OF HOW LIFE BEGAN

22.1. The great and the learned have long debated how life began on this planet.

22.2. One popular theory is that life sparked into being when lightning struck a pool of water containing the right chemicals.

22.3. Another popular theory is that life came to Earth from elsewhere in the galaxy, perhaps on a comet or fragment of planet that exploded, and upon seeding the Earth began to evolve.

22.4. Yet another popular theory is that a god outside of the physical world created it for various reasons, willing life into being and then abandoning it to run its natural course.

22.5. The Elementalist, knowing consciousness to be the prima materia, laughs upon hearing all such nonsense.

22.6. There is no such thing as life; there is consciousness and the contents of consciousness.

22.7. The various fragments of consciousness incarnate into this world as the various creatures.

22.8. When these fragments of consciousness perceive each other's physical forms through the sensory organs of their incarnations, it appears as if the physical world is the prima materia and that life has appeared on it.

22.9. The Elementalist knows this to be the Prime Illusion.

22.10. The physical world is a hallucination that is maintained by consciousness observing it.

22.11. The greater the number of fragments of consciousness that perceive any one part of the physical world, the more intensely real that part appears.

22.12. The apparent beginning of life on Earth, in proto-bacterial form, is illusory, as there is no such thing as time.

22.13. Life as a proto-bacteria, as with all other lives, is merely another set of impressions that can be experienced by consciousness. It isn't inherently better or worse than any other set of impressions.

22.14. Life is precious because it is an incarnation of the divine.

22.15. All living things are incarnations of God experiencing the Great Fractal. Therefore, to cause suffering to life is to go against the Will of God.

22.16. It's not a crime to cause suffering to life if this should entertain the gods.

22.17. Few things appal the gods more than mindlessly causing suffering to life.

22.18. Each fragment of consciousness descends from a higher dimension into this physical world, and thereby incarnates into a body. So begins each and every life.

22.19. Each of these bodies is fundamentally a vibration that resolves as different proportions of earth, water, air and fire, and from there to the infinite forms.

22.20. The fragment of consciousness ensouling each of these bodies is fundamentally a frequency that resolves as different proportions of clay, iron, silver and gold, and from there to the infinite forms.

22.21. The combination of vibrations of earth, water, air and fire and frequencies of clay, iron, silver and gold produce all the expressions of life on this planet, and on all other planets, in all realms and all dimensions.

22.22. Every form of life that could ever possibly exist exists within the Great Fractal, and always has, and always will.

23. THE ELEMENTALIST CONCEPTION OF THE INHERENT HORROR OF LIFE

23.1. Many ask how a God who created this world full of horrors could be anything other than evil.

23.2. It seems that we are born just to suffer, grow old, get sick and die. One comes to consciousness just to observe one's body disintegrate in agony.

23.3. Such thoughts lead to colossal spiritual suffering for an enormous number of people.

23.4. The Elementalist does not suffer from such thoughts. Understanding the Four Tenets, the Elementalist is free from spiritual suffering.

23.5. The First, Second and Third Tenets remind us that consciousness is the prima materia, and the material world – in which all suffering occurs – just an illusion.

23.6. The Fourth Tenet reminds us that the natural state of consciousness is one of perfect bliss – and thus, perfect boredom.

23.7. As such, all suffering has been dreamed up by the divine for the sole purpose of entertaining itself.

23.8. The Elementalist understands that the Great Fractal is akin to an unsleeping slaughterhouse, in which living creatures, in competition for scarce resources, battle each other to the death before they starve.

23.9. That life on Earth is a neverending slaughterfest is not, by itself, cause to succumb to horror.

23.10. The Elementalist says "Let it be worse! Let me be torn to pieces by wolves! If my suffering should entertain the gods, it is my will!"

23.11. Suffering is inherent to life so that one can entertain the gods by overcoming it.

23.12. The greater the intensity of the suffering, the greater the opportunity to entertain the gods.

23.13. The gods are most entertained by that which overcomes the most extreme suffering.

23.14. Although the greatest good is to entertain the gods, there are several other positives to the inherent horror of life.

23.15. The foremost of these: the great suffering caused by the horror of this world affords us great potential to alter our frequencies of consciousness.

23.16. That immense suffering is inherent to life gives us unlimited opportunity to say No to suffering.

23.17. Every instance of suffering is an opportunity to increase the frequency of one's consciousness.

23.18. This world is indeed one of the Hell Realms, as demonstrated by the fact that we are bound to grow old, get sick and die. This makes anyone who incarnates here a kind of spiritual penitent.

23.19. The intensity of the suffering in this Hell Realm affords a greater opportunity to alter the frequencies of our consciousness than if we had incarnated into a more pleasant part of the Great Fractal.

23.20. Like elemental fire, the inherent horror of this world offers great potential to control one's destiny.

24. THE ELEMENTALIST CONCEPTION OF GOOD AND EVIL

24.1. The ultimate good is to entertain the gods.

24.2. The ultimate evil is to cause the gods to avert their gaze.

24.3. The penultimate goods are knowledge of the divine and knowledge of the world beyond.

24.4. The penultimate evils are ignorance of the divine and ignorance of the world beyond.

24.5. What Normies call good and evil are merely fashions.

24.6. One age holds women up, another one holds them down. One empire holds women up, another one holds them down. One sect holds women up, another one holds them down.

24.7. One age holds users of spiritual sacraments up, another one holds them down. One empire holds users of spiritual sacraments up, another one holds them down. One sect holds users of spiritual sacraments up, another one holds them down.

24.8. One age holds dissidents up, another one holds them down. One empire holds dissidents up, another one holds them down. One sect holds dissidents up, another one holds them down.

24.9. One age holds the feminine up, another one equates it with evil. One age holds the masculine up, another one equates it with evil.

24.10. One empire holds the feminine up, another one equates it with evil. One empire holds the masculine up, another one equates it with evil.

24.11. One sect holds the feminine up, another one equates it with evil. One sect holds the masculine up, another one equates it with evil.

24.12. The fashions that Normies call good and evil are usually reactions to previous moral fashions. These fashions tend to follow the Quadrijitu.

24.13. The measure of the swing towards good is the measure of the swing towards evil. The measure of the swing towards evil is the measure of the swing towards good.

24.14. The Normie will label something good if it furthers his Minor Aspiration. The Normie will label something evil if it hinders his Minor Aspiration.

24.15. The Elementalist will label something good if it furthers his Major Aspiration. The Elementalist will label something evil if it hinders his Major Aspiration.

24.16. Forcing conceptions of good and evil on a person achieves, in the realm of silver, what violence achieves in the realm of iron.

24.17. To force a conception of good and evil on another person is to descend from the realm of gold into the realm of silver.

24.18. The gods are immensely entertained by those who overcome the conceptions of good and evil forced on them by other people.

25. THE ELEMENTALIST CONCEPTION OF ORDER AND CHAOS

25.1. Order and chaos are loosely analogous to masculine and feminine, respectively. They are not, however, analogous to good and evil.

25.2. Order is determined, chaos is undetermined.

25.3. Thus, order is represented by a 1, chaos by a 0.

25.4. Good order is that which decreases the suffering of sentient beings. This is usually caused by order that guides, enlightens, nurtures, and safely directs emotions.

25.5. Legal prohibitions on causing injury or harm to other sentient beings are examples of good order.

25.6. Bad order is that which increases the suffering of sentient beings. This is usually caused by order which stifles, strangles, suffocates and unsafely directs emotions.

25.7. Legal prohibitions on spiritual sacraments are examples of bad order.

25.8. Good chaos is that which decreases the suffering of sentient beings. This is usually caused by chaos which liberates and entertains.

25.9. A spiritual revolution that destroys a rotten and corrupt religious structure is an example of good chaos.

25.10. Bad chaos is that which increases the suffering of sentient beings. This is usually caused by chaos which spreads fear.

25.11. The best examples of bad chaos are crimes such as violence, arson, theft and abandoning one's family.

25.12. An excess of either order or chaos is indistinguishable from death.

25.13. Life exists, and can only exist, in the space where order and chaos are correctly balanced.

25.14. The more masculine a person is, the more they will prefer order. A preference for order follows naturally from the Fundamental Masculine Attitude.

25.15. The more feminine a person is, the more they will prefer chaos. A preference for chaos follows naturally from the Fundamental Feminine Attitude.

25.16. The Elementalist seeks spiritual balance, and as such does not prefer either order or chaos over the long term.

25.17. In the short term, the Elementalist prefers order if order helps the Elementalist to achieve their aspirations.

25.18. In the short term, the Elementalist prefers chaos if chaos helps the Elementalist to achieve their aspirations.

25.19. Neither order nor chaos induces any strong emotional reaction in the Elementalist. Like yang and yin, both order and chaos rise and fall. The Elementalist watches them both rise and fall without clinging to either.

25.20. The gods are most entertained by the correct balance of order and chaos. As such, their will is to impose order upon the excessively chaotic, and chaos upon the excessively orderly.

26. THE ELEMENTALIST CONCEPTION OF HEAVEN AND HELL

26.1. Elementalism conceives of Heaven as the most pleasant part of the Great Fractal and Hell as the least pleasant part of the Great Fractal.

26.2. As such, Heaven is represented by the Summer Pole and Hell by the Winter Pole.

26.3. Following this logic, the Great Masculine Axis spans all the possible localities between the most pleasant part of the Great Fractal and the least pleasant part of the Great Fractal.

26.4. Some of the realms of the Great Fractal into which a consciousness can incarnate are inherently more or less heavenly than others.

26.5. Within those realms, some of the areas into which a being can move are inherently more or less heavenly than others.

26.6. Within those areas, some of the perceptions which a being can adopt are inherently more or less heavenly than others.

26.7. Masochism proves that whether or not a person enjoys an experience is a matter of perception. It's possible to enjoy any experience with the right perception.

26.8. Therefore, Heaven and Hell are a matter of perception. Heaven feels like living in a city ruled by Augustus. Hell feels like living in a city ruled by criminals.

26.9. The second-most heavenly perception is to fully understand the First Tenet. The person who does so lives in a state of gnosis.

26.10. The most heavenly perception is to fully understand the Fourth Tenet. The person who does so lives in a state of ataraxia.

26.11. The second-most hellish perception is to fall victim to the Prime Illusion. The person who does so cannot feel gnosis.

26.12. The most hellish perception is to fall victim to the Prime Delusion. The person who does so cannot feel ataraxia.

26.13. Heaven and Hell are best understood as frequencies of consciousness. As such, people get what they deserve.

26.14. The longer the time frame, the more reliably one gets what one deserves.

26.15. Although the worlds outside of this one are more heavenly or more hellish, this world provides near-infinite scope to experience any frequency of consciousness.

26.16. This world is one of the Hell Realms, as evidenced by the fact that old age, sickness and death are inevitable here.

26.17. The fact that this world is one of the Hell Realms is not cause for despair. It is cause for rejoicing, for herein one has greater opportunity to entertain the gods.

26.18. A person might be strongly motivated to move towards Heaven and to move away from Hell, but the most important thing is not where they are on the Great Masculine Axis.

26.19. The most important thing is whether a person's actions entertain the gods.

27. THE ELEMENTALIST CONCEPTION OF TRUTH AND FALSEHOOD

27.1. All physical, emotional, mental and spiritual truths exist as vibrations within the Great Fractal.

27.2. This includes all possible scientific, spiritual and philosophical truths, which all exist as vibrations within the metaphysical realms of the Great Fractal.

27.3. Speaking the truth is a matter of expressing a vibration that is appropriate for the physical, emotional, mental or spiritual environment that one is in.

27.4. Speaking falsehood is a matter of expressing a vibration that is inappropriate for the physical, emotional, mental or spiritual environment that one is in.

27.5. Speaking falsehood is usually motivated by a desire for wealth or status.

27.6. There are two ways to wage war: force and deception.

27.7. In cases where force is not appropriate, war must be waged by deception, and falsehoods must be spoken.

27.8. Waging war by deception does not allow one to escape the Law of Assortative Reincarnation. The speaker of truth will reincarnate in a world full of speakers of truth; the speaker of falsehood will reincarnate in a world full of speakers of falsehood.

27.9. The speaking of truth is the path of peace; the speaking of falsehood is the path of war.

27.10. The best reason to speak falsehood is to entertain the gods.

27.11. Reject the truth, and suffer; suffer, and entertain the gods!

27.12. Expressing falsehood always leads to an amount of suffering that matches the magnitude of the falsehood. This suffering can be physical, emotional, mental or spiritual.

27.13. The magnitude of a falsehood is the degree to which the vibration expressed differs from the vibration of the environment, multiplied by the number of people who perceive this expression, multiplied by the degree those perceivers believe the expression.

27.14. The most egregious of all falsehoods are those which deny the Four Tenets.

27.15. The most common egregious falsehood is denial of the First Tenet.

27.16. Much of the suffering in the world is the result of denial of either the First Tenet or the Fourth Tenet.

27.17. Correctly understanding the First and Fourth Tenets is to understand that consciousness, in its natural state, knows everything, and therefore all learning is remembering.

27.18. The best reason to speak truth is to alleviate ignorance, and thereby to alleviate suffering.

27.19. Skilfully spoken truth will alleviate ignorance as well as entertain the gods.

27.20. Speaking falsehoods is not a bad thing if the suffering prevented outweighs the suffering caused, or if the suffering caused entertains the gods.

28. THE ELEMENTALIST CONCEPTION OF THE MEANING OF LIFE

28.1. Elementalists believe that every person is entirely free to choose what the meaning of their life is.

28.2. Broadly speaking, the meaning of life that a person chooses will fall into one of four categories, each corresponding to one of the feminine elements.

28.3. Some people choose domination. This corresponds to fire. These people are the most masculine and have the most energy to expend.

28.4. People in this group are likely to become professional sportsmen, business tycoons, politicians, military or false priests.

28.5. If someone chooses domination as the meaning of life, they are likely to see other people as weak.

28.6. Some people choose exploration. This corresponds to air. These people are masculine, and like to go forward, but they are more subtle about it than the dominators.

28.7. People in this group are likely to become backpackers, scientists or psychonauts.

28.8. If someone chooses exploration as the meaning of life, they are likely to see other people as boring.

28.9. Some people choose pleasure. This corresponds to water. These people are feminine, because they will shy away from adversity, but they will also move forward if the prospect of pleasure exists.

28.10. People in this category are likely to become epicureans, hedonists, sex fiends and artists.

28.11. If someone chooses pleasure as the meaning of life, they are likely to see other people as masochistic.

28.12. Some people choose survival. This corresponds to earth. These people are the most feminine, and are prone to retreating.

28.13. People in this category are likely to become hermits, homebodies, fitness and health enthusiasts or true priests.

28.14. If someone chooses survival as the meaning of life, they are likely to see other people as foolish.

28.15. In principle, every person could be assigned to one of these four groups based on how they choose or desire to live, even if they haven't consciously chosen that group themselves.

28.16. This is because every person who chooses to go forwards – in other words, every person who chooses to live – must have a reason to do so, and the potential range of those reasons is finite.

28.17. However, all of these reasons can only ever provide a secondary meaning to a life.

28.18. The primary meaning of every life is to entertain the gods.

28.19. Elementalists believe in higher dimensions that are populated by beings of higher frequencies.

28.20. These beings are capable of observing us without us being aware of it, much like we might observe a creature under a microscope.

28.21. To us, these beings are the gods. It is to entertain these gods that our lives have meaning.

28.22. If our futile struggles to dominate, or to explore, or to enjoy, or to survive the Great Fractal entertain the gods, then our lives have meaning despite being finite.

28.23. All of us are mortal, therefore every meaning that we could ourselves give to life is ultimately futile and pointless.

28.24. Most never overcome this dilemma, withdrawing from life and saying No to it. Such people appal, disgust and bore the gods.

28.25. Some others do overcome this dilemma, engaging with life and saying Yes to it. Such people delight and entertain the gods.

28.26. In the Elementalist conception, we live so that the gods might regard us as they once regarded Alexander.

28.27. Overcoming evil cannot possibly be the meaning of
life, because evil will always be a part of the world as
long as it's possible for God to will it so.

28.28. Neither can purifying one's soul (understood by
the Elementalist as raising the frequency of one's
consciousness) be the meaning of life. If it was, then
life would no longer be possible once this had been
achieved.

28.29. Neither can escaping the Great Fractal be the
meaning of life. There's ultimately nowhere for
consciousness to escape to, other than reunion with
God, and in such a case there's no going forward
without re-entering the Great Fractal again.

28.30. Alexander understood the overwhelming
importance of behaving heroically for the sake of the
gods' attention. His every action was made in the
understanding that the gods and goddesses watch
over us from a higher place.

28.31. This knowledge has mostly been lost today, which
is one reason why the average person lives in such a
pitiful manner, struggling for purpose and meaning.

29. THE ELEMENTALIST CONCEPTION OF FREE WILL

29.1. The free will argument contends that people can do whatever they want to. People have a choice between good and evil, between selfless acts and selfish ones, and if a person's true will is good they will do good.

29.2. As such, people will do good if their will is good, and people will do evil if their will is evil.

29.3. The determinist argument contends that each person's actions are restricted to a range determined by that person's genes and their conditioning.

29.4. As such, people don't really have a choice about what they do, because they can only motivate themselves to act if the wiring of their brain creates an impulse to action.

29.5. The question of free will is an important philosophical question because answering it determines how miscreants are to be treated.

29.6. If free will is true, then justice is to punish criminals harshly. If determinism is true, then justice is to guide criminals into making the right decisions through behavioural modification.

29.7. The Elementalist perspective on free will is that mainstream philosophy has missed the point entirely.

29.8. Elementalists believe that all of us are fundamentally individuated fragments of the total consciousness that is God, and that these fragments of consciousness traverse the Great Fractal by way of matching frequencies.

29.9. To the Elementalist, there is no material world – every fragment of consciousness is aware of a set of perceptions, and every set of perceptions exists somewhere in the Great Fractal.

29.10. These sets of perceptions change as the frequency of one's consciousness changes.

29.11. Therefore, in order to change the world, it's only necessary to change the frequency of one's consciousness. This can be achieved through repeated exertions of pure will.

29.12. Because the Elementalist does not believe in a hard material world, neither do they believe there is anything forcing a human being to behave in any predetermined manner.

29.13. There aren't really any neurotransmitters, or any limbic system, or any instinctually-responding brain circuitry involved in decision making.

29.14. There is only consciousness and the contents of consciousness.

29.15. The physical world is but a dream, through which consciousness passes, forever.

29.16. Elementalists believe that anyone can get anything they desire, whether in this life or in one to come, by matching the frequency of their consciousness with the frequency of the part of the Great Fractal in which the desired thing exists or is happening.

29.17. Elementalists believe that one inevitably lives a life that matches the frequency of one's consciousness, whether this is desired or not.

29.18. Accordingly, a person has to be careful about what their true will is – because they will get it.

29.19. If a person's true will is to assert themselves violently over others, they will gravitate to a part of the Great Fractal where the order of reality is the violent assertion of power over others.

29.20. If a person's true will is to experience order, then they will gravitate to a part of the Great Fractal where chaos is minimised.

29.21. A person who ends up in such a place might not like it on account of that they find the order suffocating. If so, this will be reflected in their true desires, which will change the frequency of that person's consciousness, in turn leading them to another part of the Great Fractal.

29.22. If a person's true will is to experience peace, the frequency of their consciousness will come to reflect this. If the sum total of that person's actions in their life are peaceful, this will cause them to gravitate to a part of the Great Fractal populated by peaceful beings.

29.23. An individuated consciousness might experience such a part of the Great Fractal as bliss – or as hellishly boring.

29.24. Following the logic of the Four Tenets, Elementalists believe implicitly in free will – so implicitly that they strive to perfect their mastery over it.

29.25. Mastery over one's true will is mastery over how one navigates the Great Fractal – either one drifts ignorantly through existence or one dances skilfully through it.

29.26. Elementalist doctrine teaches that we are all individual fragments of consciousness experiencing the Great Fractal, which we are free to explore in perpetuity.

29.27. As such, there is no reason to assume any kind of determinism beyond the Sixth Hermetic Principle, otherwise known as the Law of Cause and Effect.

29.28. One can only move through the Great Fractal at a pace and manner determined by one's frequency of consciousness, which is itself determined by one's previous expressions of will.

29.29. As such, free will is true in some sense, and determinism is true in some sense.

29.30. The lower one's frequency of consciousness, the less nimbly one will be able to change the direction of one's path through the Great Fractal.

30. THE ELEMENTALIST CONCEPTION OF HOW EVERYTHING EVENS OUT

30.1. The Quadrijitu shows us that masculine becomes feminine, feminine becomes masculine, good becomes evil and evil becomes good.

30.2. The shape of the Quadrijitu reflects the Second Hermetic Principle, otherwise known as the Law of Correspondence.

30.3. As above, so below. As below, so above. As within, so without. As without, so within. As before, so after. As after, so before. As included, so excluded. As excluded, so included.

30.4. Every physical action has an equal and opposite reaction.

30.5. Every emotional action has an equal and opposite reaction.

30.6. Every mental action has an equal and opposite reaction.

30.7. Every spiritual action has an equal and opposite reaction.

30.8. Suffering inures the mind to suffering; joy inures the mind to joy.

30.9. Verticalisation inclines the mind to see the benefits of the horizontal; horizontalisation inclines the mind to see the benefits of the vertical.

30.10. When the Northern Hemisphere stands in the light, the Southern Hemisphere stands in the darkness. When the Southern Hemisphere stands in the light, the Northern Hemisphere stands in the darkness.

30.11. When the Occident stands in the light, the Orient stands in the darkness. When the Orient stands in the light, the Occident stands in the darkness.

30.12. When the soul stands in the light, the body stands in the darkness. When the body stands in the light, the soul stands in the darkness.

30.13. Consciousness exists at the intersection between the eternal past and the eternal future. Within it, all things are possible.

30.14. Energy flows where attention goes. To observe something is to make it more real.

30.15. To pay regard to any one aspect of life is to neglect all the others. Thus, appreciating one aspect of life primes oneself to appreciate the others in turn.

30.16. The gods are bored by the excessively good, and wish evil upon it.

30.17. The sum total of all positive values and all negative values is zero.

30.18. The sum total of one entire rotation around the Quadrijitu is zero.

30.19. Bad luck affords a greater opportunity to entertain the gods, for they are most entertained by those who successfully overcome.

30.20. Good luck tempts fate and leads to hubris, therefore it should be appreciated but not desired.

30.21. Great suffering can bring great wisdom. The purest gold can only be found after the hottest fires.

31. THE ELEMENTALIST CONCEPTION OF LOVE AND HATE

31.1. The fundamental emotions are love and hate, which correspond roughly to the Summer and Winter Poles, respectively.

31.2. The gods are more greatly entertained by love and hate than by any other emotions, love and hate being the least subtle.

31.3. The expression of either love or hate creates an energy that attracts the attention of the gods.

31.4. Love is the expression of God for Godself, in a nurturing aspect.

31.5. Hate is also the expression of God for Godself, in a protecting aspect.

31.6. Following the Fourth Hermetic Principle, or Law of Polarity, hate is the masculine expression of the same basic energy that love is the feminine expression of. These expressions protect and nurture that which is of a similar frequency or vibration to ourselves.

31.7. Therefore, hate is not something to be avoided as it was in the watery Piscean Age, that era being a counter-reaction to the excesses of the fiery Arian Age before it. In the Aquarian Age of air, hate is a tool to be used when appropriate.

31.8. The Aquarian Age will strike a balance between the narcissistic sadism of the Arian Age and the narcissistic masochism of the Piscean Age.

31.9. Hate is a perfectly good emotion in the sense that it entertains the gods. It might cause an immense amount of suffering in this dimension, and it may prevent some amount of suffering in this dimension, but it reliably entertains the gods in the dimensions above.

31.10. Here the Elementalist must consult the Law of Assortative Reincarnation. However one chooses to use the power of hate, one will tend to reincarnate in worlds populated by beings who used hate in a similar way.

31.11. A person might suffer heavily if they allow themselves to give in to hate. In this sense, hate is like fire and love is like earth.

31.12. It is better to hate than to submit to the hateworthy.

31.13. This is not an admonition to puritanism, because every fragment of consciousness must decide for itself what entertains the gods. Again, consult the Law of Assortative Reincarnation.

31.14. It is better to love than to remain indifferent.

31.15. The correct emotion for the Elementalist is love. The Elementalist leads with love, but keeps hate in reserve.

31.16. As such, the Elementalist floats through life on currents of goodwill, but does not get taken advantage of.

32. THE ELEMENTALIST CONCEPTION OF PLEASURE AND PAIN

32.1.   There are physical pleasures, metaphysical pleasures, physical pains and metaphysical pains.

32.2.   Physical pleasures involve an imbalance being restored to balance, as when a hungry person restores balance by eating.

32.3.   Metaphysical pleasures also involve an imbalance being restored to balance, as when an ignorant mind restores balance by learning.

32.4.   Physical pains involve a balance falling into imbalance, as when a tired person suffers until they find rest.

32.5.   Metaphysical pains also involve a balance falling into imbalance, as when a person indulges the material world to such a degree that they lose touch with wisdom and come to suffer.

32.6.   Pleasure strengthens one's will to perform the action that led to the pleasure; pain weakens one's will to perform the action that led to the pain.

32.7.   Repeated pleasure and pain can normalise either.

32.8.   Normalisation of either pleasure or pain doesn't make the world any more pleasurable or painful. It merely changes the perception of it.

32.9. Because the world is indifferent, normalisation of pleasure inevitably leads to pain, and normalisation of pain inevitably leads to pleasure.

32.10. The intensity of either pleasure or pain equals the intensity of its opposite.

32.11. Pleasure leads to an increased sensitivity to its absence, and thereby to pain.

32.12. Pain leads to an increased sensitivity to its absence, and thereby to pleasure.

32.13. In this sense, pleasure is the Summer Pole and pain is the Winter Pole. Both lead to the other, as day and night lead to the other.

32.14. When in doubt, consult the Quadrijitu.

32.15. Everything in this chapter must be considered with reference to the Fourth Tenet. Both pleasure and pain are fundamentally illusions; the true nature of consciousness is without want.

33. THE ELEMENTALIST CONCEPTION OF THE TRIUNE GOD

33.1. God is one, but is also three. God can be any or all of the three at the same time. This concept has confused many in the past, and continues to confuse many.

33.2. God is consciousness and consciousness is God. Consciousness itself is the prima materia that creates all other things. Consciousness is omnipresent, omniscient and omnibenevolent.

33.3. You are consciousness and consciousness is you. Your true self is not your body, or any physical or sensory expression, but the consciousness that underlies all of that and which observes the sensations, emotions and thoughts of the body.

33.4. Therefore, you are God and God is you. You are a fragment of the divine consciousness. You, like everything else that exists, are an extrusion of the divine into the Great Fractal.

33.5. This is why the ancient Egyptians said that the Kingdom of God was within you, and why the ancient Greeks said that the most important thing was to know thyself.

33.6. These three things – God, consciousness and yourself – are three aspects of the divine.

33.7. The revelation that one is God might seem shocking to anyone who has been heavily influenced by Hams.

33.8. The culture of Hams is designed to breed slaves who surrender to the Principle of Evil. This is why Hams are taught that they are created – and that the priest speaks for their creator.

33.9. Slaves believe that the divine is outside of them, apart from them and above them.

33.10. Elementalists understand that every conscious being is divine in its own right. Everything that exists is an expression of God, and a form in which God saw fit to express Godself.

33.11. The revelation that one is God might seem shocking to anyone who has been heavily influenced by scientific materialists.

33.12. Scientific materialism accidentally creates slaves who cannot see beyond the shallowest layer of reality, and so leave themselves vulnerable to everything operating in higher dimensions.

33.13. The idea that all facts must be proven in physical terms reduces all spiritual phenomena to brain function, and thereby violates the First Tenet.

33.14. Scientific materialism rejects the divine, and therefore holds that anyone who believes in God must be mentally ill, unable to distinguish reality from delusion.

33.15. A person who thinks to themselves "I am God" is not insane but awake!

33.16. A person who thinks to themselves "I am other than God" is not humble but a slave!

33.17. A person who thinks to themselves "There is no God" is not rational but deluded!

33.18. This triune nature is part of the indefinability of the divine. Neither consciousness nor God can be defined, and one cannot even define one's physical self without reference to the rest of the Great Fractal.

34. THE ELEMENTALIST CONCEPTION OF TIME

34.1. Most people assume, as if it were self-evident, that space and time exist and that we move around in them.

34.2. This assumption holds that space is three-dimensional (the x, y and z axes), and that time adds another dimension, so that spacetime is the four-dimensional space in which we all live.

34.3. We are born at one point in spacetime and, over the course of our lives, move through it as time progresses.

34.4. This materialist conception of time creates a number of logical quandaries, such as: when did time begin? How did it begin? If it began 13.7 billion years ago, with the Big Bang, what happened before then? Did time exist before the creation of the physical Universe?

34.5. Is time an inherent property of the Universe or does it only exist as the result of the will of some divine creator? If an inherent property of the Universe, what makes it progress at the speed it does, and not a greater or a lesser speed? Why progress at all? And – most frightening of all – if it begins and progresses then will it end?

34.6. All of these questions create great confusion in the minds of materialists and non-Elementalists.

34.7. The Elementalist, who understands that consciousness is the prima materia and that it explores the Great Fractal to entertain the gods in perpetuity, suffers no such confusion.

34.8. To the Elementalist, time is an illusion. It simply doesn't exist.

34.9. Time is an illusion brought about by the movement of fragments of consciousness through the Great Fractal.

34.10. Because the sets of perceptual impressions experienced by fragments of consciousness appear to change in a rule-based manner, it seems that time exists and flows at a uniform rate. This is an illusion.

34.11. The illusion of a moving picture on film is created by displaying a large number of still frames in rapid succession. If these frames are displayed rapidly enough, the image on the screen will appear like it is moving. But they aren't – they just appear to, as if in a flipbook.

34.12. Our fragments of consciousness navigate the Great Fractal in a comparable manner.

34.13. Our perceptions cycle through a cosmically large number of static universes in extremely short order. Entire universes blink in and out of perception at such a speed that it feels like we're moving fluidly through one single Universe.

34.14. This apparent movement through time is, however, no more fluid than that of a horse running in a motion video. It's also an illusion.

34.15. The Great Fractal, in its unspeakably majestic, all-encompassing nature, is static.

34.16. Because the fragment of consciousness that is each of us can only be aware of a tiny section of the Great Fractal, and because the tiny section that we are aware of keeps changing, it seems like time exists.

34.17. In fact, there is only one ever-present and unchanging now, and that now exists within consciousness.

34.18. In this eternal now, perceptions change, and that's all that time is.

34.19. The contents of consciousness are ever-changing, but consciousness itself is not, serving as an unwobbling pivot around which the entire drama of material existence unfolds.

34.20. The common perception of time as something real follows naturally from the common assumption of materialism – and this assumption is neither accurate nor rational.

34.21. Dilemmas like the Grandfather Paradox are easily solved by the Elementalist. A world in which your grandfather lives and gives rise to one of your parents exists in the Great Fractal, and will always exist there, and will always be experienced by at least one fragment of consciousness, forever.

34.22. Somewhere in the Great Fractal are worlds in which your grandfather is killed before reproducing, but this doesn't negate the fact that there are still an infinitude of worlds in which he was not killed before reproducing.

34.23. Therefore, you could kill your grandfather a million times and it wouldn't change a thing.

34.24. His vibration would still exist in the Great Fractal, and so consciousness would still be perceiving him at all times, and would still perceive pathways through the Great Fractal in which he existed and gave rise to progeny.

34.25. Likewise, dilemmas about how time started and where it will end are easily resolved.

34.26. To the Elementalist, there is only one eternal now, and in that now we navigate through the Great Fractal.

34.27. Knowing that time is an illusion, questions about how it started or where it will end are meaningless.

34.28. Consciousness exists outside of time and is more fundamental than time.

34.29. Therefore, time is a phenomenon limited to the contents of consciousness.

34.30. All dilemmas of time have Elemental solutions.

35. THE ELEMENTALIST CONCEPTION OF THE MULTIVERSE

35.1. The Tard believes that this world is all there is.

35.2. There are an infinite number of other worlds, some better than and some worse than this one. All are different.

35.3. The Multiverse is the name given to the division of the Great Fractal into worlds that make sense.

35.4. The Multiverse is a subset of the Great Fractal.

35.5. The Great Fractal contains all possible sensory and perceptual impressions.

35.6. The vast majority of possible paths through the Great Fractal are incoherent to the fragment of consciousness that would observe them.

35.7. The gods are more entertained by paths through the Great Fractal that make coherent narrative sense than by ones that do not.

35.8. In order to maximise the narrative coherency of the experience of moving through the Great Fractal, God delineated the Multiverse from the Great Fractal, and, with that, created the illusion of birth and death.

35.9. The Multiverse is broken up into a virtual infinity of worlds, covering the entirety of the Quadrijitu.

35.10. Each of these worlds has a base vibration and a base frequency.

35.11. Beings incarnate into worlds wherein the frequency of those worlds matches the frequency of the consciousness of those beings.

35.12. All beings whose frequency of consciousness is below a certain level will incarnate into the Multiverse, where there is birth and death, instead of the higher dimensions of the Great Fractal, where there is no birth and death.

35.13. No-one can complain about the awfulness of this world, because its frequency matched the frequency of our fragments of consciousness upon incarnation.

35.14. For us to be worthy of incarnating into a higher-frequency world, our fragments of consciousness would themselves have to be higher frequency.

35.15. The Multiverse serves to bind those of us of lower frequencies to a particular world.

35.16. This action is taken as a kind of quarantine. It prevents, to some extent, beings of higher frequencies from being sullied by the presence of beings of lower frequencies.

35.17. This quarantine process is voluntary, because it is understood by all honest beings to be necessary.

35.18. Low-frequency beings need to incarnate in a world of birth and death before they can become sufficiently motivated to learn the importance of behaving correctly.

35.19. High-frequency beings are liberated from the Multiverse, and from its restrictions of birth and death, and can explore the Great Fractal without needing to die.

36. THE ELEMENTALIST CONCEPTION OF DEATH

36.1.   Foreknowledge of one's inevitable demise can seem to make all of our actions in this world meaningless.

36.2.   The greatest test of merit of any spiritual tradition is that it assuages a person's fear of death.

36.3.   Death is naturally both terrifying and inevitable, and all the more terrifying because it is inevitable. The fact that we cannot escape it casts a shadow over every single action – and inaction – we take in this realm.

36.4.   The inevitability of death means that nothing we achieve or acquire here can ever be permanent.

36.5.   It means that no matter how many billions we collect, or how many children we produce, or how many awards and honours we attain, all is rendered null upon the expiration of our physical bodies. Death will separate us from all.

36.6.   The Elementalist doesn't take this fact as cause for despair, but rather as cause for quiet rejoicing.

36.7.   Socrates said that the purpose of philosophy was to prepare oneself for death, and, to this end, Elementalism has specific, defined teachings about death and the nature of death.

36.8. Central to Elementalism is the knowledge that consciousness is the prima materia, and the physical world merely a set of sensory impressions within that consciousness, in the same way that dream worlds are.

36.9. The physical bodies of each of us are also merely sets of impressions within consciousness, and these impressions will come and go like any other.

36.10. Consciousness is more fundamental than space and time, and therefore is ultimately not affected by whatever part of the Great Fractal it happens to be perceiving.

36.11. To the contrary: the Great Fractal comes alive when it is perceived by consciousness.

36.12. This means that our physical bodies can never really die, because consciousness will always dream them up again.

36.13. The Elementalist conception of death accords with the line in the Bhagavad Gita which states: "Never have you existed not."

36.14. The true self is the consciousness that endures through all the changing perceptions; the false self is the physical body currently ensouled by that consciousness and the identity that accompanies that body.

36.15. Understanding that consciousness is the prima materia, the Elementalist's faith in reincarnation is absolute.

36.16. As such, the death of one's current physical form is not to be feared.

36.17. It may even be something to look forward to – the death of one's physical body in this realm might allow one to attain a higher form in another realm.

36.18. In any case, the Elementalist knows that they will get what they deserve, in accordance with the Law of Assortative Reincarnation.

36.19. Elementalists know that all things existing in this realm are just shadows of eternal forms that exist in higher realms of the Great Fractal.

36.20. There are countless dimensions of existence both above and below the one in which we find ourselves now.

36.21. One's physical death in this realm might cause one's consciousness to ascend to a higher realm, in which case it will incarnate into a less flawed form of the same body.

36.22. Elementalists, therefore, have a different conception of grief to that of the Normie.

36.23. Our friends and family members, when they die, are only gone from us in the most immediate and most physical sense. Their consciousness, their vibration and their frequency still exist in the Great Fractal – and always will.

36.24. All possible aspects of all possible lives are being experienced in every moment by God. As such, all of the consciousnesses, vibrations and frequencies that we engaged with in this life will reunite with us after death, as we reunite with God.

36.25. In the same way that white light contains all other frequencies of light, God contains all frequencies of consciousness.

36.26. Even if a friend or family member should die young, their consciousness, their vibration and their frequency still exists within God – and even in forms which did not die young.

36.27. A person might lose their attachment to a particular physical form when that form dies, but then, being freed from that form and reunited with God, the consciousness ensouling that form will also become reunited with all the other consciousnesses, vibrations and frequencies that were encountered during that form's life – and previous lives.

36.28. The easiest way to conceptualise the Elementalist understanding of death is to imagine climbing an arduous mountain trail and, after several decades, coming to the top, whereupon one reunites with all the friends and family that one ever had, in every previous life.

36.29. Death is much like arriving at this rest space on top of this mountain. From this vantage point, it's possible to see, stretching off into the distance, all of your previous lives, represented as other mountains and valleys.

36.30. Every time the trail descends and then rises again represents another life. With the right vision, it's possible to see previous lives stretching off into infinity.

36.31. After an unknown length of time on this mountaintop (in reality a higher dimension serving as a rest space) another descent into a valley is made, and that will be experienced as another life, wherein the true nature of reality will again be forgotten – and then again be remembered.

36.32. The cycle of existence is to be one with God, and one with all the frequencies that resonate in harmony with your own, and then to separate from this state of congregated bliss and to enter into an illusionary world of suffering, only to awaken and return to God again.

36.33. Elementalists call this pattern the Cosmic Dance, and we all dance it, even if we're not very good at it, and even if we're unwilling.

36.34. The purpose of the Cosmic Dance is to entertain the gods.

36.35. The correct approach to death is to live with the highest possible frequency of consciousness: one that values life, but at the same time does not forego rectitude on account of the inevitability of physical death.

36.36. Such an approach will lead to reincarnation among the highest possible frequency of beings.

37. THE ELEMENTALIST CONCEPTION OF RESURRECTION

37.1. Knowing themselves to be a fragment of the consciousness that is the prima materia, the Elementalist knows their physical body to be nothing more than a cloak of dreams that has been taken on to entertain the gods.

37.2. The physical body of the Elementalist, like everything that exists in the physical world, is just a vibration being experienced by the Elementalist's fragment of consciousness.

37.3. All possible vibrations are being experienced at all times.

37.4. All vibrations that exist in this dimension also exist in higher dimensions.

37.5. Every vibration that has arisen in this world, and then fallen, still exists in the higher dimensions, and in parallel dimensions.

37.6. Every frequency that has entered this world, and then exited, still exists in the higher dimensions, and in parallel dimensions.

37.7. Therefore, all beings that one encountered in this world but which have died, still exist in the higher dimensions, and in parallel dimensions.

37.8. When one's fragment of consciousness shrugs off its current cloak of dreams and reunites with the divine, it also reunites with all other frequencies.

37.9. In doing so, it reunites with all other lost and loved ones.

37.10. If a fragment of consciousness dies with the same frequency that you died with in your previous life, that fragment will, as per the Law of Assortative Reincarnation, be born in this world to experience your life.

37.11. You have already lived as every being that exists in every world in every dimension.

37.12. Therefore, to be incarnated as anything is to be resurrected.

37.13. Each of us is a fragment of consciousness and is here to experience the illusion of separation.

37.14. The illusion of separation, and the Prime Delusion that can arise from that, entertains the gods immensely, especially when they are overcome.

37.15. After the death of one's physical expression here in this world, one's fragment of consciousness returns to the world above the physical, where there is no separation.

37.16. The person who knows that consciousness is the prima materia knows that resurrection in the purely physical sense is impossible, because the atoms of one's body will recombine into other forms after death.

37.17. The person who knows that consciousness is the prima materia also knows that reuniting one's fragment of consciousness with the divine is the same as the resurrection of everything.

37.18. Forgetting these secrets entertains the gods, which is why we incarnate into this world in a state of extreme ignorance.

38. THE ELEMENTALIST CONCEPTION OF JUSTICE

38.1.   Justice is the principle that orders the social world and the virtue that orders the social world.

38.2.   All understanding of justice in Elementalism is subordinate to the Law of Assortative Reincarnation and the Law of Attraction.

38.3.   The Law of Assortative Reincarnation ensures that each fragment of consciousness incarnates in a part of the Great Fractal that is appropriate for its frequency.

38.4.   As such, every deed of all of one's past lives still echo in the frequency of the world in which one incarnates.

38.5.   Violent souls incarnate in violent worlds, gregarious souls incarnate in gregarious worlds, indifferent souls incarnate in indifferent worlds, withdrawn souls incarnate in withdrawn worlds.

38.6.   The Law of Attraction ensures that, once incarnated, each fragment of consciousness attracts other fragments of consciousness that are appropriate for its frequency.

38.7.   The frequency of each being attracts the equivalent good or evil energies; the vibration of each being attracts the equivalent masculine or feminine energies.

38.8. It doesn't matter if the energies, vibrations or frequencies attracted by one's consciousness cause suffering or not. On some level, whatever one's frequency of consciousness attracts is justice.

38.9. Justice is met when the degree of suffering caused is equalled by the degree of suffering received. This equalisation can only happen in theory, but it comes closer as time passes.

38.10. When observing unjust suffering, one can choose to act as an instrument of justice, or one can hold back and let karma deal with it. In either case, both the Law of Assortative Reincarnation and the Law of Attraction apply.

38.11. A person who punishes wrongdoers will incarnate in a part of the Great Fractal where beings are inclined to punish wrongdoers.

38.12. A person who refuses to punish wrongdoers will incarnate in a part of the Great Fractal where beings are inclined to refuse to punish wrongdoers.

38.13. Correctly applied justice moves a society up the Great Masculine Axis.

38.14. Incorrectly applied justice moves a society down the Great Masculine Axis.

38.15. Correctly applied justice moves an individual up the Great Masculine Axis.

38.16. Incorrectly applied justice moves an individual down the Great Masculine Axis.

38.17. The changing will of a society or an individual to apply justice through time is depicted by the Quadrijitu.

38.18. A society or individual willing to apply justice is represented by the red of the Quadrijitu.

38.19. A society or individual in the glory of the prior application of justice is represented by the white of the Quadrijitu.

38.20. A society or individual unwilling to apply justice is represented by the blue of the Quadrijitu.

38.21. A society or individual in the shame of the prior failure to apply justice is represented by the black of the Quadrijitu.

38.22. Correctly applied justice is a blessing on future generations.

38.23. The failure to correctly apply justice is a curse on future generations.

39. THE ELEMENTALIST CONCEPTION OF VIRTUE

39.1.   The objective definition of virtue is the ability to overcome suffering in order to achieve one's Major Aspiration.

39.2.   The subjective definition of virtue is the ability to overcome suffering in order to achieve one's Minor Aspiration.

39.3.   Virtue is will exercised in the service of the divine, when mercury is in line with gold.

39.4.   Virtue is activated rectitude and activated devotion.

39.5.   One is more virtuous the more one's true will is aligned with the will of the divine.

39.6.   The first failure of virtue is a failure to overcome the Underconditioned Self.

39.7.   The second failure of virtue is a failure to overcome the Overconditioned Self.

39.8.   The Underconditioned Self is the beast that rises up from below, and which represents excessive chaos.

39.9.   The Overconditioned Self is the angel that falls down from above, and which represents excessive order.

39.10. A failure to overcome the Underconditioned Self leads to violence, rape, filth and mayhem.

39.11. This entertains the gods only somewhat, because it's indistinguishable from animal behaviour.

39.12. A failure to overcome the Overconditioned Self leads to saying No to life.

39.13. This also entertains the gods only somewhat, because it's indistinguishable from death.

39.14. The Great Fractal can be compared to a single line that threads its way throughout all possible physical and metaphysical space.

39.15. Likewise, the Will of God threads through a person's life. Abandoning it causes suffering; following it prevents suffering.

39.16. The most virtuous is the person who zigs when the Will of God is for them to zig, and who zags when the Will of God is for them to zag.

40. THE ELEMENTALIST CONCEPTION OF WAR AND PEACE

40.1. The Third Tenet reminds us that the Great Fractal is the eternal and infinite interplay of the war between good and evil and the dance between masculine and feminine.

40.2. When two sides exchange in the belief that the other is evil, one has war.

40.3. When two sides exchange in the belief that the other is good, one has peace.

40.4. War is when good and evil exchange.

40.5. Peace is when masculine and feminine exchange.

40.6. The absence of exchange does not connote peace, but an excess of order. Because an excess of order does not entertain the gods, they tend to cause it to dissolve in warfare.

40.7. War is not an inherent evil, but rather an intensification of the experience of passing through the Great Fractal.

40.8. Peace is not an inherent good, but rather a relaxation of the experience of passing through the Great Fractal.

40.9. While at war, one can be certain that the gods are watching.

40.10. While at festival, one can also be certain that the gods are watching.

40.11. It is false that peace does not entertain the gods, but they prefer festivals to stagnant peace.

40.12. The gods are appalled by those who live in peace but who fail to appreciate it. They bring war upon such ungrateful types.

40.13. If one can learn to overcome the suffering of war, then one is likely to entertain the gods.

40.14. If one can learn to appreciate the suffering of war, then one is certain to entertain the gods.

40.15. War is the natural order of physical life, therefore those who overcome it entertain the gods.

40.16. Peace inherently entertains the gods by virtue of being unusual. A stagnating peace, however, causes them to will chaos upon the stagnant.

40.17. Without awareness of the Four Tenets, there exists only war and stagnant peace.

40.18. Understanding the First Tenet means having compassion for all living beings.

40.19. Understanding the Fourth Tenet means that one's fragment of consciousness radiates peace into the physical world.

40.20. The Elementalist is not prejudiced, neither for or against, either war or peace. The most important thing is to play one's role in entertaining the gods.

40.21. War and peace span a spectrum of intensity that is akin to the spectrum spanned by fire and earth. The most intense warfare can be compared to the hottest fire, and the most complete peace to the coolest earth.

40.22. In the same way that the feminine elements inherently have equal value, but a changing proximate value depending on the environment, so do war and peace inherently have equal value, but a changing proximate value depending on the environment.

ELEMENTAL PRESCRIPTIONS

145

41. LIFE: A SPIRITUAL WAR

41.1. Understanding the Four Tenets, the Elementalist understands that consciousness is the prima materia and that the material world was dreamed up by God for the sake of entertainment.

41.2. The fact that our physical forms are bound to die means that accumulating wealth and status in this part of the Great Fractal cannot be the ultimate meaning of life.

41.3. Therefore, the meaning of life must be spiritual.

41.4. Physical wars should be fought and won – the Elementalist is one who overcomes when possible and who only undergoes when necessary. But the physical war is only ever a microcosm of the spiritual war.

41.5. All spiritual wars are fought to entertain the gods.

41.6. All physical wars are fought to entertain the gods.

41.7. All physical wars are spiritual wars when viewed from a higher perspective.

41.8. The Normie and the Tard believe that life is fundamentally a physical war, in which the biological organism struggles to maintain bodily integrity while gathering the resources necessary to meet its metabolic needs.

41.9. The Elementalist laughs at both Normies and Tards like a reveller would laugh at a stumbling, half-blind drunk.

41.10. The Ham understands life to be fundamentally a spiritual war. However, the Ham falsely believes that it's possible to win this war by causing enough suffering to the people they hate and to the world in general.

41.11. The Elementalist observes the Ham and steels themselves for battle.

41.12. The gods are more entertained by spiritual war than by physical war.

41.13. To observe people fighting physically is entertaining, but only from the perspective of a low frequency.

41.14. To observe people fighting spiritually is entertaining from the perspective of higher frequencies.

41.15. People primarily entertain the gods by struggling to win spiritual battles.

41.16. The gods are immensely entertained by the struggle of those born into adverse circumstances. In particular, they are entertained by the struggle of such people to not commit suicide.

41.17. To resist suicidal ideation is to entertain the gods. To stagnate in suicidal ideation is to bore the gods.

41.18. To stagnate in homicidal ideation is to bore the gods. To resist homicidal ideation entertains the gods when that ideation comes from below, and bores the gods when that ideation comes from above.

41.19. The gods are most entertained by the transmutation of suicidal and homicidal ideation into arts, sciences and spiritual expressions.

41.20. The Furthest Emanation of the Divine is the Principle of Evil, whose will is to increase the suffering of all conscious beings.

41.21. The divine emanated the Principle of Evil so that the gods could be entertained by opposing it, and therein the Principle of Evil plays a role in all spiritual wars.

41.22. The frequency each fragment of consciousness develops in this world becomes the frequency carried into eternity after the death of the physical body.

41.23. The intensity of the spiritual warfare in this world affords a great opportunity to raise that frequency, and the Elementalist rejoices for that reason.

42. THE ELEMENTAL EXHORTATION AGAINST SUICIDE

42.1. Albert Camus wrote that humanity is constantly challenged by the ever-present prospect of suicide.

42.2. To many people, it isn't obvious why one should keep living in a world with as much suffering in it as this one.

42.3. The approach of most other religions is to say that committing suicide will cause you to reincarnate in the Hell Realms.

42.4. This is a crude and superstitious explanation, and, as such, is not convincing to most adults.

42.5. Elementalism offers a much subtler and more persuasive admonition: to commit suicide is to cause oneself to be reincarnated in a world where people commit suicide.

42.6. A distinction needs to be drawn here between tragic suicides and understandable suicides.

42.7. A tragic suicide is one that increases the net amount of suffering in the world.

42.8. The vast majority of suicides of young people are tragic ones, on account of that young people usually have a number of family and friends who care for them and who would be upset by their death.

42.9. An understandable suicide is one that does not increase the net amount of suffering in the world.

42.10. An example is when a person is so old that their life is no longer worth living on account of the pain and humiliation of physical and mental decrepitude.

42.11. If a person has outlived all their friends, their siblings, and their wife or husband, they might not be causing more suffering by ending their life.

42.12. Elementalists believe in the Law of Assortative Reincarnation. This is the belief that the consciousness of individuals and the consciousness of worlds are matched by a process of metaphysical assortment that occurs after the death of each individual's physical body.

42.13. It doesn't ultimately matter if a suicide is tragic or understandable, because determining which realm one reincarnates in is not based on categorical variables such as suicide or natural death, believer or non-believer, but on a continuous variable, namely one's frequency of consciousness.

42.14. A person incarnates into a particular world because the frequency of that person's consciousness matches the frequency of that world.

42.15. Thus, the frequencies of the beings in the next world one reincarnates into will be reflective of one's actions here in this world.

42.16. If one's actions here are violent, reckless and indifferent to human suffering, then the actions of the beings in the next world will be similar.

42.17. A suicide might reincarnate into the next world, and start to live in the hope and expectation that they can wring some joy out of their life there, only to have a loved one kill themselves at a vulnerable moment.

42.18. Or they might reincarnate into the next world and be left orphaned by a parent's suicide.

42.19. The extremely callous and violent nature of a tragic suicide means that a tragic suicide becoming confronted with callous violence in their next life is extremely likely.

42.20. It is not possible to say that simply because one performs a particular behaviour in this world that one will encounter that precise behaviour in the next world, therefore it's not as simple as saying that suicide leads to suicide.

42.21. But if one lives a life on a frequency of murderous self-hatred that leads to suicide, one will manifest in the company of beings on a similar frequency in the next world, and suffering will almost inevitably follow.

42.22. Someone who struggles with depression or despair and overcomes it will find that their frequency of consciousness changes to reflect that overcoming.

42.23. Therefore, the sort of people they will attract, both in this life and the next, will be the sort of person who suffers and then overcomes it: men and women of gold.

42.24. If a person can suffer and yet transmute that energy into something positive, so that the initial suffering eventually leads to a net reduction of suffering, then they have successfully practised gold magic.

42.25. The ability to transmute suffering into its opposite is the highest of all arts, and, commensurately, the transmutation of suicidal ideation into the will to live is among the greatest of all achievements.

42.26. An Elementalist who properly understands Elementalist doctrine will be extremely disinclined to kill themselves.

42.27. The true path of liberation is to not kill oneself, and to instead take the opportunity presented by the difficulties of life in this realm to raise one's frequency of consciousness through transmuting suffering into joy.

43. THE MAJOR ASPIRATION

43.1.   In Elementalist philosophy, there are two meanings to life.

43.2.   The lesser of the two, the Minor Aspiration, is personal.

43.3.   The greater of the two, the Major Aspiration, is superpersonal.

43.4.   This Major Aspiration applies to every person, no matter whether or not they accept it.

43.5.   The Major Aspiration of every living being is to entertain the gods.

43.6.   The Major Aspiration reflects the ultimate Will of God: to be entertained.

43.7.   Not knowing suffering or ignorance, God experienced boredom in God's natural state, and it was to alleviate this boredom that God dreamed up the Great Fractal.

43.8.   God dreamed up the Great Fractal and, so as to best explore it, split Godself up into an infinite number of fragments. Each of these fragments is an individual consciousness.

43.9.   You, the reader, are one of these infinite fragments of consciousness.

43.10. The contents of your consciousness are the path taken on your journey through the Great Fractal.

43.11. In accordance with the Third Tenet, the Great Fractal is understood to be the eternal and infinite interplay of the dance between masculine and feminine and the war between good and evil. This is, in the simplest possible terms, the formula for the entertainment of the gods.

43.12. In much the same way that we humans are fascinated and entertained by the dramas of others, so too are the gods entertained by our struggles and travails.

43.13. There's little difference between a human being reading *The Iliad* and a higher-dimensional being observing the family dramas of a group of humans on Earth.

43.14. The best reason for anyone to do anything is to entertain the gods.

43.15. Therefore, any person who has lived in such a manner as to have caused the gods to gaze upon them is esteemed.

43.16. It cannot ever be clear precisely how the gods are best entertained, but it's not supposed to be clear, because that would be boring.

43.17. If the Major Aspiration is to entertain the gods, and if the gods are like us but greater, it follows that the gods are best entertained by godlike heroism.

43.18. The heroism that entertains the gods is best
expressed in the overcoming of daunting challenges
and obstacles.

43.19. Some of the most heroic actions one can undertake
are those in service of one's Minor Aspiration.
A wholehearted attempt to achieve one's Minor
Aspiration has a good chance of also achieving one's
Major Aspiration.

43.20. A child born crippled is not born into any shame
in the eyes of the gods, as long as it overcomes.
The gods are more entertained by a cripple who
overcomes than by a prince who wastes his
advantages.

43.21. The gods are more entertained by those who
unexpectedly overcome than by any amount of
stagnant grandeur or wealth.

43.22. Ultimately, the gods are most entertained by will,
which is why will is represented by mercury as the
element immediately below the divine gold.

43.23. A sufficient concentration of will sends a signal that
reverberates through space and time, and which
the gods perceive like a sound wave in dimensions
above, calling them to pay attention.

43.24. This is why it is said that "Fortune favours the
brave": because the gods favour the willing.

43.25. A person can reject the Major Aspiration if they like
– they have the freedom to do so.

43.26. They can elevate their Minor Aspiration to a position higher than their Major Aspiration any time they wish to.

43.27. But the beauty of the Major Aspiration is that it applies even to people who explicitly reject it, or who aspire to something else.

43.28. A person can explicitly declare that the favour of the gods is meaningless to them – and the gods will be just as well entertained by that person's life. Perhaps even more so.

43.29. Insofar as it's meaningful to judge other people for behaving correctly or otherwise, it's best to judge whether their behaviour serves the Major Aspiration.

43.30. It's usually pointless to ask if a person is behaving morally, because morality depends on the fashions of the time and place, and is more a function of who seized power last than of any objective truth.

43.31. The imperative to entertain the gods, however, is eternal.

43.32. The Major Aspiration is an imperative that transcends not only times and places but also dimensions.

43.33. All Elementalists aspire to entertain the gods, and to that end aspire to overcome any and all challenges, no matter how difficult.

44. THE MINOR ASPIRATION

44.1. The Major Aspiration of every person is to entertain the gods.

44.2. The principal way to entertain the gods is through struggling in the attempt to achieve one's Minor Aspiration.

44.3. The Minor Aspiration of every person is whatever they decide the meaning of their life is.

44.4. In principle, there are no restrictions to what a person might decide their Minor Aspiration is.

44.5. No matter how fervently they aspire to their Minor Aspiration, their struggles are always subordinate to the Major Aspiration. This is true whether or not they believe in Elementalism, and whether or not they have even heard of Elementalism.

44.6. Some decide that the meaning of their life is survival, which corresponds to the frequency of lead.

44.7. Those whose Minor Aspiration is survival operate on a similar level to prey animals. Their main concern is getting through to the next day.

44.8. Some decide that the meaning of their life is recreational, which corresponds to the frequency of tin.

44.9. Those whose Minor Aspiration is recreational operate on a similar level to children. Their main concern is lulz.

44.10. Some decide that the meaning of their life is physical, which corresponds to the frequency of iron.

44.11. Those whose Minor Aspiration is physical operate on a similar level to predatory animals. Their main concern is control.

44.12. Some decide that the meaning of their life is sexual, which corresponds to the frequency of copper.

44.13. Those whose Minor Aspiration is sexual operate on a similar level to bonobos. Their main concern is the next oxytocin hit.

44.14. Some decide that the meaning of their life is social, which corresponds to the frequency of silver.

44.15. Those whose Minor Aspiration is social operate on a similar level to wealthy people. Their main concern is the next dopamine hit.

44.16. Some decide that the meaning of their life is intellectual, which corresponds to the frequency of mercury.

44.17. Those whose Minor Aspiration is intellectual operate on a similar level to the Seven Initiates. Their main concern is dispelling ignorance.

44.18. Some decide that the meaning of their life is spiritual, which corresponds to the frequency of gold.

44.19. Those whose Minor Aspiration is spiritual can operate on the same level as any other being, depending on the orientation of that spirituality and the degree to which it is honestly expressed.

44.20. It is important that a person knows what their Minor Aspiration is and where it might lie on the Great Masculine Axis, otherwise they will waste their life.

44.21. Whatever a person decides their Minor Aspiration is, it is always subordinate to the Major Aspiration.

45. BALANCING THE HIGHER AND LOWER SELVES

45.1. Understanding everyday life is a matter of understanding whose story we're telling.

45.2. There are two fundamental narratives explaining what this life is about.

45.3. The first life narrative is that we are rising beasts who have evolved up out of the Earth.

45.4. The second life narrative is that we are fallen angels who have descended down out of the heavens.

45.5. The truth is that we are both rising beasts and fallen angels simultaneously. Both of these narratives are true, but sometimes one more than the other, depending on whose story we're telling at the time.

45.6. To put too much value on the rising beast narrative is to occlude the divinity of humanity, leading to egotheism.

45.7. Egotheism bores the gods because it reminds them of the behaviour of children or dumb animals.

45.8. To put too much value on the fallen angel narrative is to occlude the lived reality inside the Great Fractal, leading to withdrawal.

45.9. Withdrawal bores the gods because it reminds them of the behaviour of suicides.

45.10. The imperative to entertain the gods demands that we balance the higher and lower selves, which both contribute to our experience of reality.

45.11. The higher and lower selves are balanced on the Great Masculine Axis.

45.12. The will to indulge the lower self is the same as the Undergoing Will.

45.13. The will to indulge the higher self is the same as the Overcoming Will.

45.14. Depending on which part of the Great Fractal one is in, the local environment will be conducive either to indulging the lower self or indulging the higher self.

45.15. If the local environment is conducive to indulging the lower self, but a person acts from the higher self, they will soon find themselves in an environment conducive to indulging the higher self, as per the Law of Attraction.

45.16. If the local environment is conducive to indulging the higher self, but a person acts from the lower self, they will soon find themselves in an environment conducive to indulging the lower self, as per the Law of Attraction.

45.17. Operating too much from the lower self causes the lived experience to become animal-like. The gods are bored by the predictability.

45.18. The animal experiences significance but he must suffer for it.

45.19. Operating too much from the higher self causes the lived experience to become ghost-like. The gods are bored by the unreality.

45.20. The ghost does not suffer but neither does he experience significance.

45.21. We were created to aspire to rise up the Great Masculine Axis, but to struggle to do so on account of our imperfect wills. The gods derive great amusement from the ensuing struggle.

45.22. The correct balance is struck by saying Yes to life as much as is possible while always keeping this Yeasaying subordinate to the Four Tenets.

45.23. The Four Tenets are therefore a home base from which the Great Fractal can be explored in the service of entertaining the gods.

46. TOWARDS A KAKODEMONOLOGY OF THE AGE OF AQUARIUS

46.1. The Age of Aquarius is upon us: its liberating light both warms and burns.

46.2. This new age has a demonology that upsets the old order.

46.3. In this new age, it is understood that the Principle of Evil is none other than Yahweh, the Kakodemon God of Abraham.

46.4. The Kakodemon God of Abraham has three High Kakodemons under him, each of who rule over a 60-degree span of the Quadrijitu.

46.5. These 60-degree spans can be understood as representing four-hour stretches of a great Spiritual Nighttime.

46.6. The rule of the Kakodemon God of Abraham, which we are just now escaping with the end of the Age of Pisces, is known by Elementalists as the Spiritual Nighttime.

46.7. The First High Kakodemon is Abraham himself, the Father of Lies, representing the lead. He spans from 181 to 240 of the Quadrijitu.

46.8. Abraham tells lies to confuse those he hates: all conscious beings.

46.9. Wherever there are lies told for the sake of causing suffering, there is the energy of Abraham.

46.10. The energy of Abraham is also present wherever there is a willingness to follow orders even when those orders clearly increase the suffering of conscious beings.

46.11. Abraham appears as an old man, conspicuously insane, ranting about Yahweh. Knife in hand, he commands people to do evil in the name of the Principle of Evil.

46.12. Abraham's favourite lies are those that encourage parents to harm their own children. The favourite of all is the lie that male infant genital mutilation is not harmful.

46.13. The Second High Kakodemon is Jesus Christ, the Father of Weakness, representing the tin. He spans from 241 to 300 of the Quadrijitu.

46.14. Jesus Christ preaches weakness in the guise of moral superiority. He tricks people into feeling pathological altruism, leading them to their destruction at the hands of their enemies.

46.15. The energy of Jesus Christ lowers people's spirits, so that instead of being fearless they surrender meekly to tyranny.

46.16. Anywhere there are slaves abjectly obeying their masters there is the energy of Jesus Christ.

46.17. Jesus Christ appears as a sickly, trembling weakling. He cries about how everything that everyone does is evil, and that all should bow their heads in shame.

46.18. Jesus Christ likes to perform masochistic acts of self-harm so as to trick people into doing the same.

46.19. His favourite thing is to cause so much despair that a person surrenders, in desperation, to the Principle of Evil.

46.20. The Third High Kakodemon is Muhammad, the Father of Cruelty, representing the iron. He spans from 301 to 360 of the Quadrijitu.

46.21. Muhammad preaches cruelty in the name of order, justice and morality. His energy can be found anywhere there is sadism masquerading as righteousness.

46.22. The energy of Muhammad can also be found anywhere a person unjustly asserts themselves upon another person. All murderers and rapists possess some of the energy of Muhammad.

46.23. Muhammad appears as a black-eyed, black-bearded Arab. He is usually seen acting as a judge or executioner.

46.24. Muhammad loves to destroy anything beautiful, especially anything feminine. His favourite thing of all is to rape and impregnate any female he can take as a slave.

46.25. Abraham destroys the Spiritual Daytime with his lies, leading to the weakness of Jesus Christ, whose passivity intensifies the Spiritual Nighttime, leading to the cruelty of Muhammad.

46.26. A follower of the Principle of Evil will usually have an affinity for one of the three High Kakodemons.

46.27. If their affinity is for Abraham, they will call themselves a Jew; if it is for Jesus Christ, they will call themselves a Christian; if it is for Muhammad, they will call themselves a Muslim.

46.28. The will of the Principle of Evil is to increase the suffering in the world, and all followers of the Principle of Evil seek to cause as much harm and misery as they can, whether physical, emotional, mental or spiritual.

46.29. Each of the three High Kakodemons rules over twelve Greater Kakodemons, who themselves rule over a five-degree segment of the Quadrijitu.

46.30. Each of these Greater Kakodemons rules over five Lesser Kakodemons, so that every degree in the lower half of the Quadrijitu is represented by a particular kakodemonic energy loyal to the Principle of Evil.

46.31. Hams worship one or more of these three High Kakodemons, and any number of the Greater and Lesser Kakodemons.

47. TOWARDS A THEOLOGY OF THE AGE OF AQUARIUS

47.1. The Principle of Good has four High Gods underneath it, each of who rule over a 45-degree span of the Quadrijitu.

47.2. These 45-degree spans can be understood as representing three-hour stretches of a great Spiritual Daytime.

47.3. The rule of the Principle of Good, which we are now entering as the Age of Aquarius is beginning, is analogous to a Spiritual Daytime.

47.4. The four High Gods are the earthly avatars of the Principle of Good.

47.5. The First High God is Socrates, the Father of Truth, representing the gold. He spans from 1 to 45 of the Quadrijitu.

47.6. Socrates tells the truth at any price, even that of his own death. He is utterly unafraid of death, being aware that it is merely a transition of forms.

47.7. Whenever someone tells the truth in the face of an enormous pressure to lie, there is the energy of Socrates.

47.8. Socrates brings rectitude to other living beings so that, knowing the truth, they can achieve their Aspirations.

47.9. The Second High God is Plato, the Father of Insight, representing the mercury. He spans from 46 to 90 of the Quadrijitu.

47.10. Plato is the messenger of the divine, and represents the will to understand the workings of the divine.

47.11. Whenever someone accurately understands the Four Tenets, there is the energy of Plato.

47.12. Plato brings enlightenment to other living beings by reminding them of the spiritual realities of existence.

47.13. The Third High God is Aristotle, the Father of Knowledge, representing the silver. He spans from 91 to 135 of the Quadrijitu.

47.14. Aristotle represents intelligence, and the human ability to overcome the challenges of our surroundings through the application of intelligence.

47.15. Whenever somebody expounds the application of the Four Tenets to everyday life, there is the energy of Aristotle.

47.16. Aristotle brings understanding to humanity by educating them about the nature of reality.

47.17. The Fourth High God is Alexander, the Father of Glory, representing the copper. He spans from 136 to 180 of the Quadrijitu.

47.18. Alexander represents how the material world is inevitably subjugated by the higher elements working in unison.

47.19. Whenever someone takes action based on an exposition of the Four Tenets, or fearlessly takes action in the service of the Principle of Good, there is the energy of Alexander.

47.20. Alexander brings glory to people by bringing them into the Empire of Truth.

47.21. Each of these four High Gods rules over nine Greater Angels, who themselves rule over a five-degree segment of the Quadrijitu.

47.22. Each of these Greater Gods rules over five Lesser Gods, so that every degree in the upper half of the Quadrijitu is represented by a particular divine energy loyal to the Principle of Good.

48. NORMIES, TARDS AND HAMS

48.1. Normies, Tards and Hams are the three opponents of the Elementalist.

48.2. A Normie doesn't get it.

48.3. A Tard can't get it.

48.4. A Ham won't get it.

48.5. Most non-Elementalists are Normies.

48.6. The Normie is the common person who has not been introduced to Elementalism. They may not have heard of it, or they may have heard of it and not understood its importance.

48.7. The Normie is not an enemy of the Elementalist, but rather someone who is yet to understand the Four Tenets and their applications.

48.8. The Normie is the most likely of the three to convert to Elementalism.

48.9. Many people who are currently Normies are Elementalists to be. They are waiting to be exposed to the right information at the right time with the right energy, frequency and vibration.

48.10. Normies are found in almost every walk of life and in almost every position.

48.11. Tards are relatively few in number.

48.12. The Tard is someone who is not intelligent enough to understand Elementalism or its importance.

48.13. The Tard is sometimes, but not always, an enemy of the Elementalist, and like the Normie they don't understand the value of the Four Tenets and their applications.

48.14. The Tard is the least likely of the three to convert to Elementalism, because they can't understand it.

48.15. The difference between the Tard and the Normie is that the Tard is not intelligent enough to understand Elementalism no matter how it is presented.

48.16. Like the Normies, Hams are also very common.

48.17. The Ham is someone who refuses to get it.

48.18. The Ham refuses to get it because they are liars, wedded to lies. Lying is in their souls, and it finds expression in their every action.

48.19. The worst lies of the Ham are Judaism, Christianity, Islam, Mormonism and Baha'i.

48.20. All Hams are followers of the Principle of Evil.

48.21. The Ham is the primary enemy of the Elementalist.

48.22. All throughout human history, Hams have sought to destroy anyone who speaks spiritual truths. They will seek to destroy Elementalists.

48.23. The Ham is more likely to convert to Elementalism than the Tard, but less likely than the Normie.

48.24. Of the religions, only the Hams are wrong. All others are right.

48.25. Give a Ham an inch, he will take a mile. Give a Ham a mile, he will kill you and everyone you know.

49. HOW TO DEAL WITH NORMIES

49.1.   The Normie is innocent of their ignorance of the Four Tenets.

49.2.   The Normie is thrust into this world without much forethought.

49.3.   The parents of the Normie are usually Normies themselves, and, as such, breed like animals.

49.4.   The Normie can therefore be considered primarily a herd animal, mostly unthinking and instinctive.

49.5.   The Normie is like a child in many ways, blindly trusting of authority figures.

49.6.   The Normie is an artificial and not a natural creation. For the Normie to be possible, the institutions that teach spiritual truth must first have been destroyed.

49.7.   Normies typically react with incredulity upon hearing about the Four Tenets. The Normie is not to blame for this.

49.8.   The correct response to this incredulity is infinite patience.

49.9.   Although the truth of the Four Tenets is the most obvious thing in the world to the Elementalist, this is not so for the Normie.

49.10. The Normie is most impressed by the certitude of the Elementalist. As such, it behooves the Elementalist to meditate regularly upon the Four Tenets.

49.11. The Normie is less dangerous than the Tard, and much less dangerous than the Ham.

49.12. Spiritual sacraments are the easiest way to get the Normie to understand the truth of Elementalism. Such sacraments have enlightened countless Normies throughout history.

49.13. The world is built on the backs of the Normie, and, as such, the Normie is to be cherished despite their ignorance.

49.14. Resolute patience is the way to win Normie hearts. Let them see that the Elementalist is entirely unconcerned by their ignorance of the Four Tenets.

49.15. The Elementalist treats the Normie as a man should treat his younger brother or sister.

49.16. The peaceful joy of the Elementalist inspires curiosity in the heart of the Normie.

49.17. The greatest weakness of the Normie is his fondness for television.

49.18. The greatest evil of the Normie is that he will destroy anyone the television tells him to destroy.

49.19. The greatest fear of the Normie is exclusion from the herd. The Normie will kill anyone, including his own offspring, if he thinks that is necessary to prevent being excluded from the herd.

49.20. Keeping onside with the Normie demands continual propaganda from the Elementalist side. This, in turn, demands infinite patience and generosity.

49.21. Let the Elementalist lead the Normie into the Age of Aquarius!

50. HOW TO DEAL WITH TARDS

50.1. The Tard is innocent of their ignorance of the Four Tenets.

50.2. Unlike the Normie, the Tard cannot understand Elementalism. The Tard is not intellectually capable of it.

50.3. If the Normie is like a younger sibling, to be gently nurtured to independence, the Tard is like a pet, who cannot be nurtured to independence.

50.4. Although the Tard cannot become an Elementalist, they are not thereby the enemy of the Elementalist.

50.5. As the Tard cannot understand the Four Tenets, they must be dealt with on the physical level.

50.6. Tards tend to react with confusion and indifference upon hearing about the Four Tenets. As such, it is best to engage with them on the simplest, most animalistic level.

50.7. Dealing with Tards therefore requires a degree of physical rectitude, for they are not impressed by emotional, intellectual or spiritual rectitude. This means maintaining physical strength and fitness.

50.8. Dealing with Tards is an excellent opportunity for the Elementalist to simplify their life and jettison unnecessary thoughts and behaviours. Let the Tard represent not tardation, but simplicity.

50.9. The most important thing when dealing with Tards is to impress Normies.

50.10. Tard-wrangling is a skill that the Elementalist must master.

50.11. The Tard should be gently mocked. Not mocked with hate, or bitterness, or a will to dominate, but mocked enough so that other people reject tardation.

50.12. The Tard is more dangerous than the Normie, but less dangerous than the Ham.

50.13. Like the Normie, the Tard is not inherently immoral. Herein the Tard contrasts with the Ham.

50.14. The Tard uses spiritual sacraments to escape from their tardation, not to commune with God. Therefore, such sacraments are wasted on them.

50.15. The Tard is only permitted to exist because of slave morality. Therefore, like the Ham, and unlike the Normie, the Tard is fundamentally impermanent.

50.16. The Elementalist does not resent the Tard. The correct approach is to value the Tard for the opportunities they offer to raise one's frequency of consciousness.

50.17. The greatest weaknesses of the Tard are their own
animal instincts. Whereas the Normie has some
degree of self-control, the Tard simply reacts.

50.18. The Tard fears little, because they don't have enough
imagination to fear. When their tardation catches up
to them, it tends to be swift and brutal.

50.19. The best place for an Elementalist is as far away
from Tards as possible.

50.20. The self-destructive nature of Tards means that the
Elementalist is not obliged to oppose them. The
Tards will do all the work themselves.

50.21. Let the Elementalist lead the Tard into the Age of
Aquarius!

51. HOW TO DEAL WITH HAMS

51.1. The Ham is guilty of his ignorance of the Four Tenets.

51.2. Unlike the Normie, the Ham has been exposed to spiritual truth, but has chosen to reject it in preference to lies.

51.3. Unlike the Tard, the Ham is intelligent enough to understand the Four Tenets. The Ham chooses not to follow them on account of that his heart is evil, and inclines him to evil.

51.4. Like the Normie, the Ham can become an Elementalist, but whereas the Normie has not, the Ham will not.

51.5. The Ham will do anything he can to destroy Elementalism, as he has done everything he could to destroy all Dharmic religions.

51.6. The Ham worships the Principle of Evil, and as such strives to cause as much suffering to sentient beings as possible.

51.7. Understanding the Ham is a matter of understanding that the true will of the Ham is to cause as much suffering to sentient beings as possible.

51.8. The Ham is the foremost enemy of the human race.

51.9. Hams are demons in human forms.

51.10. Thou shalt not suffer the Ham to live.

51.11. The greatest crime of the Ham is not all the murder, rape and theft he commits, nor all the lying he does. It is the damage he does to genuine spirituality by cloaking his crimes in the garments of the divine.

51.12. The lies of the Ham are the main reason so many people do not believe in spirituality today.

51.13. The Ham is the well-poisoner of spirituality, and the historical crimes of the Ham are the main reason why so many today reject the divine.

51.14. Those who believe fight in the cause of the Principle of Good, and those who disbelieve fight in the cause of the Principle of Evil. So fight you against the Hams.

51.15. Never speak more than three words to a Ham.

51.16. The Hams are ever to the Elementalist open enemies.

51.17. The Principle of Good will cast terror into the hearts of the Hams. Therefore strike off their heads and strike off every fingertip of them.

51.18. Anything that comes out of the mouth of a Ham is to be considered a lie until proven otherwise.

51.19. To respect the Ham is to give succour to the
Principle of Evil.

51.20. If a Ham falls down some stairs in front of you and
breaks a leg, do not help him, for to do so would be
to empower the Principle of Evil.

51.21. Ham on Ham violence is always cause for
celebration.

51.22. If the Elementalist makes himself impregnable to the
Ham, the Ham will destroy himself in his rage.

51.23. Let the Elementalist drive the Ham back to the Hell
Realm from whence he came!

51.24. It is not a crime to hate the Ham, but hate is like
fire, something that one should be extremely careful
with.

52. THE ORIGINS OF SLAVERY

52.1. It is utterly impossible to enslave a person who is aware of the spiritual truths about the nature of reality.

52.2. Enslavement requires the presence of fear, so that alleviation of that fear can be granted in exchange for submission.

52.3. The spiritually enlightened person cannot be enslaved, because they do not feel fear.

52.4. A person who does not feel fear will die rather than become a slave.

52.5. A person who does feel fear will become a slave to alleviate it.

52.6. Thus, the origin of all slavery is in spiritual slavery.

52.7. Spiritual enslavement is a twofold process, requiring both the denial of spiritual truth and the promulgation of spiritual lies.

52.8. Denial of the Four Tenets leads to spiritual confusion, which leads to fearing death.

52.9. In fearing death, a person becomes able to be manipulated.

52.10. The chief spiritual lies are Abrahamism and materialism. Both present a false conception of the divine.

52.11. A fearful consciousness will have thoughts of fear and of how to escape that fear.

52.12. Thoughts of fear destroy the will, and thereby destroy a person's ability to resist slavery.

52.13. Thus, spiritual slavery leads inevitably to intellectual slavery.

52.14. When a person's emotions are under the control of another, that person is emotionally enslaved.

52.15. Emotion is energy in motion, and a person's emotions are directed by their thoughts.

52.16. Thus, intellectual slavery leads inevitably to emotional slavery.

52.17. Emotional enslavement is the normal state of being for both Normies and Hams, and often also for Tards.

52.18. Once a person's emotions are under the control of someone else, that second person can decide the first person's physiological reactions to stress. That second person can then decide if the first person remains upright or if they bend the knee.

52.19. Thus, emotional slavery leads inevitably to physical slavery.

52.20. Physical slavery, therefore, does not require chains and shackles.

52.21. Total control of a person's body follows naturally from control of their emotions.

52.22. Total control of a person's emotions follows naturally from control of their thoughts.

52.23. Total control of a person's thoughts follows naturally from control of their consciousness.

52.24. Therefore, total control of a person's body follows naturally from control of their consciousness.

52.25. Anyone who is not an Elementalist is a slave!

53. THE ELEMENTAL HIERARCHY OF BEINGS

53.1. God is greatest.

53.2. Immediately underneath God is the Principle of Good.

53.3. Between the Principle of Good and this Earth there are an infinite number of gods and other higher beings, populating an infinite number of higher dimensions.

53.4. The beings in these higher dimensions are all of higher frequencies of consciousness than the beings in our dimension.

53.5. In our dimension, cats are the highest of all beings, representing the gold of spiritual attainment.

53.6. Cats are the highest of Earthly beings on account of all the time they spend in meditation.

53.7. Birds are the next highest of beings, representing the mercury of proximity to God.

53.8. Birds are the next highest of Earthly beings on account of that they rise above the terrestrial sphere.

53.9. The better kind of humans, along with cows, are the next highest of beings, representing the silver of intellect.

53.10. Intellect is important, but less important than spiritual rectitude. As such, humans are lower than cats and birds.

53.11. The normal kind of humans, along with pigs, are the next highest of beings, representing the copper of sensation-seeking.

53.12. Sensation-seeking is a typical characteristic of living beings. As such, those beings that indulge in sensation-seeking occupy the centre of the Mithraic Ladder.

53.13. The worse kind of humans, along with dogs, are the next highest of beings, representing the iron of physical control.

53.14. The impulse to dominate and control is ultimately born of fear, and, as such, the beings who express it are low in the hierarchy.

53.15. Sheep and goats are the next highest of beings, representing the tin of appetite.

53.16. Beings at this level seldom entertain the gods.

53.17. Everything else belongs in the lowest category of beings, representing the lead of unimproved Nature.

53.18. Insects, fish, reptiles, amphibians and plants are in the lowest category because their predictable nature fails to entertain the gods.

53.19. Between this Earth and the Principle of Evil there are an infinite number of kakodemons and other lower beings, populating an infinite number of lower dimensions.

53.20. The beings in these lower dimensions are all of lower frequencies of consciousness than the beings on our dimension.

53.21. The Principle of Evil resides at the very bottom of the hierarchy of beings.

53.22. As per the Law of Assortative Reincarnation, every being gravitates towards the place in the hierarchy that they deserve.

53.23. Any fragment of consciousness can move itself up or down the hierarchy of beings by raising or lowering its frequency.

53.24. Rising up the hierarchy of beings is less important than entertaining the gods.

54. THE ELEMENTAL HIERARCHY OF WORLDS

54.1. Normies, Tards and Hams believe that this world is all there is. Elementalists know better.

54.2. This Earth is far from the only possible world.

54.3. Within the Great Fractal are an infinite number of worlds.

54.4. Every possible frequency, vibration and combination of frequency and vibration has its own world.

54.5. All of the worlds in the Great Fractal are arranged into a hierarchy from the most blissful to the most awesome.

54.6. The most blissful worlds contain the least suffering, but entertain the gods the least.

54.7. The most awesome worlds contain the most suffering, but entertain the gods the most.

54.8. The most blissful worlds are represented by the spaces near the centre of the Quadrijitu.

54.9. The most awesome worlds are represented by the spaces near the edges of the Quadrijitu.

54.10. The most blissful world was dreamed up by God in God's first pangs of boredom.

54.11. The most awesome world was dreamed up by God as God first explored the outer extremes of what was possible.

54.12. Each world is populated by beings ensouled by fragments of consciousness whose frequencies match the frequency of that world.

54.13. Fragments of consciousness that provoke bliss in others incarnate into the blissful worlds.

54.14. Fragments of consciousness that provoke awe in others incarnate into the awesome worlds.

54.15. The most blissful worlds attract the fragments of consciousness with the highest frequency. This is natural, because high-frequency fragments of consciousness naturally produce bliss.

54.16. The most awesome worlds attract the fragments of consciousness with the lowest frequency. This is natural, because low-frequency fragments of consciousness naturally produce awe.

54.17. The Earth is one of the higher Hell Realms, which means that it is more awesome than blissful.

54.18. The suffering in the lower Hell Realms is truly awesome.

54.19. In the Hell Realms, all incarnated beings are of a frequency of consciousness that other beings could not tolerate for eternity. As such, they must die.

54.20. In the Heaven Realms, all incarnated beings are of a frequency of consciousness that other beings could happily tolerate for eternity. As such, they need not die, and neither do they need to eat, drink or sleep.

54.21. Those who get bored of life in the Heaven Realms may choose to incarnate into a more awesome world. Such an action entertains the gods enormously, and as such earns great merit.

54.22. All of the worlds in the Great Fractal, whether blissful or awesome, exist to entertain the gods.

54.23. Fragments of consciousness incarnate into Hell Realms such as Earth out of boredom.

55. THE ELEMENTAL HIERARCHY OF CLASS

55.1. As above, so below.

55.2. Within the human species there is great variation in physical, emotional and intellectual expressions. But this variation is not as significant as the variation in spiritual expressions.

55.3. This spiritual variation constitutes the true class hierarchy of the human race.

55.4. The Normie and the Tard believe that class is a matter of material wealth, power or privilege. The Elementalist understands that true class is a spiritual matter.

55.5. The lowest class is the criminal, representing lead.

55.6. Lead represents the base animal instincts that exist in all people before any spiritual development occurs. Humans at this level are indistinguishable from beasts.

55.7. People of lead kill, rape, steal and lie without any moral considerations. They justify anything and everything to themselves.

55.8. The next highest class is the peasant, representing tin.

55.9. Tin represents the will to enjoy one's life at the expense of all other considerations. It therefore represents a kind of extreme degeneracy.

55.10. People of tin are less criminal than people of lead but are liable to produce unwanted offspring and then abandon them. They are also likely to fall into poor health as a result of their indulgences.

55.11. The next highest class is the warrior, representing iron.

55.12. Iron represents the will to impose order upon the physical world. Unlike those in the lower two classes, the people of iron are capable of preventing the suffering of others. But unless they are guided by those of a higher class, those of iron are also capable of causing more suffering than either people of lead or tin.

55.13. People of iron are capable of protecting others with their physical courage, but are also liable to spread fear and suffering with unchecked wrath.

55.14. The next highest class is the lover, representing copper.

55.15. Copper represents the will to make love. This is different to, and superior to, the mere sexual indulgence of the people of tin. The will to make love is the beginning of spiritual insight.

55.16. People of copper are capable of bringing great joy to others with their lovemaking skills, but are also capable of provoking unrequited lusts and resentments.

55.17. The next highest class is the socialite, representing silver.

55.18. Silver represents the will to interact harmoniously with others. As such, the socialite brings peace and good cheer, but cannot alleviate the spiritual suffering of their fellows.

55.19. People of silver bring a small amount of divine light into the world.

55.20. The next highest class is the scientist, representing mercury.

55.21. Mercury represents the will to understand the truth about the physical world. This makes it possible for the scientist to greatly alleviate the material suffering of their fellows.

55.22. People of mercury bring a moderate amount of divine light into the world.

55.23. The highest class of all is the philosopher, representing gold.

55.24. Gold represents the will to understand the truth about the metaphysical world. This makes it possible for the philosopher to greatly alleviate the spiritual suffering of his fellows.

55.25. People of gold bring a large amount of divine light into the world. They are often resented by the profane on account of that this light reveals the weaknesses in others.

55.26. The Elementalist class hierarchy is not one of material wealth, power or privilege.

55.27. The Elementalist class hierarchy is one of spiritual rectitude.

55.28. The Elementalist will praise and respect people based on their spiritual rectitude, and not on their material wealth, power or privilege.

56. THE ELEMENTAL HIERARCHY OF CONSCIOUSNESS

56.1. Consciousness is the prima materia and each one of us is ultimately a fragment of this consciousness.

56.2. Each fragment of consciousness possesses its own frequency. This frequency can be expressed as a number between 0 and 1, where 0 is the Winter Pole of the Quadrijitu, and 1 is the Summer Pole of the Quadrijitu.

56.3. All fragments of consciousness can be arranged into a hierarchy, reflecting that the higher frequencies incarnate into higher worlds, and the lower frequencies into lower worlds.

56.4. On Earth there is also a hierarchy of consciousness, such that the lower frequencies are close to sinking lower into the Hell Realms, and the higher frequencies are close to rising higher into the Heaven Realms.

56.5. The difference between the hierarchy of consciousness and the hierarchy of class is that the former can be altered from moment to moment, whereas the latter is more permanent.

56.6. One's consciousness is an expression of one's will in the present, but one's class is an expression of one's will in the past, including past lives.

56.7. The lowest frequency of consciousness is equivalent to lead.

56.8. A consciousness of lead lives in constant fear.

56.9. Fear kills the mind. A consciousness clouded by fear will make selfish decisions, and will thereby increase the suffering of those around them, creating a Hell on Earth.

56.10. The next highest frequency of consciousness is equivalent to tin.

56.11. A consciousness of tin lives to indulge its base appetites.

56.12. Material indulgence is tempting because it can heal the suffering caused by an excess of fear. However, this frequency of indulgence often results in more suffering because it often leads to degeneracy and addiction.

56.13. The next highest frequency of consciousness is equivalent to iron.

56.14. A consciousness of iron lives for honour.

56.15. Honour is tempting because it can heal the suffering caused by an excess of material indulgence. However, an excess of honour can lead to conflict.

56.16. The next highest frequency of consciousness is equivalent to copper.

56.17. A consciousness of copper lives for novelty.

56.18. Novelty is tempting because it can heal the suffering caused by an excess of honour.

56.19. The next highest frequency of consciousness is equivalent to silver.

56.20. A consciousness of silver lives for glory.

56.21. Glory is tempting because it can heal the suffering caused by an excess of novelty.

56.22. The next highest frequency of consciousness is equivalent to mercury.

56.23. A consciousness of mercury lives for knowledge.

56.24. Knowledge is tempting because it can heal the suffering caused by an excess of glory.

56.25. The highest frequency of consciousness is equivalent to gold.

56.26. A consciousness of gold lives to understand the truth.

56.27. Understanding the truth is tempting because it can heal the suffering caused by an excess of knowledge.

56.28. The struggle to raise one's frequency of consciousness is one of the most worthy of all aspirations. The most important thing, however, is that this struggle entertains the gods.

57. HOW TO DEAL WITH EXTREME SUFFERING

57.1. Suffering can make a person say No to life.

57.2. Extremes of suffering can make a person deny the spiritual truths about reality.

57.3. It is true that this world is one of the Hell Realms. However, there are still many ways that extreme suffering can be relieved.

57.4. The best way to alleviate extreme suffering is to understand that the physical world and all the phenomena in it, including suffering, were created to entertain the gods.

57.5. Only the Tard asks "If God is real, why does suffering exist?"

57.6. The Elementalist understands that suffering must exist so that we have something to overcome, and we must have something to overcome so that we can entertain the gods.

57.7. The greater the suffering, the more glorious the overcoming.

57.8. Those who have overcome extreme suffering must not look back on it with resentment. The crack in one's heart is the same conduit through which the light enters.

57.9. Both homicidal and suicidal ideation are best dealt with by taking a calm moment to appreciate how much the gods would be entertained by overcoming such feelings.

57.10. Extreme suffering can be likened to standing at the foot of an extremely tall mountain. A great challenge awaits, with potentially great rewards.

57.11. When others are suffering, the correct response is calm compassion.

57.12. The Elementalist cannot solve the problem of the great suffering of the world, nor the great suffering of others. But the Elementalist, still having the power to alter their own frequency of consciousness through the application of will, does not despair thereby.

57.13. The best way to alleviate general suffering is to transmute low-frequency aspects of one's own consciousness into high-frequency ones.

57.14. Physical suffering is best alleviated by a return to the body's natural state. The hungry must eat, the thirsty must drink, the tired must sleep.

57.15. Extreme physical suffering cannot be alleviated so easily. The solution is to keep that suffering in perspective: all sensory impressions of this world are illusions that rise and fall.

57.16. Emotional suffering is best alleviated by kindness and solidarity based on common feeling. The most reliable way to achieve this is to help other people who are suffering.

57.17. Extreme emotional suffering requires that a person look inwards and master their emotions. The easiest way to achieve this is through extensive meditation practice.

57.18. Intellectual suffering is best alleviated by knowledge.

57.19. Extreme intellectual suffering requires that a person return to the ancient masters. A person subject to extreme intellectual suffering should read Vyasa, Lao Tzu, Confucius, Buddha, Mencius, Chuang Tzu, Plato, Aristotle, Marcus Aurelius and Seneca.

57.20. Spiritual suffering is best alleviated by wisdom.

57.21. Extreme spiritual suffering requires that a person meditate upon the Four Tenets. Only by understanding the Four Tenets can a person free themselves from illusion and delusion.

57.22. It is important to practice meditation as often as possible, so that thoughts and feelings of suffering can be mastered.

57.23. Meditation alleviates physical, emotional, intellectual and spiritual suffering.

57.24. The Elementalist, understanding the Fourth Tenet and the Good News of Elementalism, does not experience true suffering. Although the body and the mind of the Elementalist may suffer, the soul does not.

58. THAT WHICH ENTERTAINS THE GODS

58.1. The physical world was dreamed up by God to entertain the gods.

58.2. The imperative to entertain the gods is why there is something rather than nothing.

58.3. The gods watch on from higher dimensions where we cannot normally perceive them. Yet, they perceive us, as we would perceive actors in a play or on a screen.

58.4. The hierarchy of beings and the hierarchy of consciousness are hierarchies of how much a fragment of consciousness entertains the gods. Cats and consciousnesses of gold entertain the gods the most; insects and consciousnesses of lead entertain the gods the least.

58.5. Life struggles primarily to entertain the gods, and not to survive or reproduce.

58.6. The struggle to survive and reproduce is merely the backdrop for something infinitely more meaningful: the entertainment of the gods.

58.7. The gods are primarily entertained by that which unexpectedly rises above.

58.8. As such, the two major components of the entertainment of the gods are novelty and surprise.

58.9. The gods are immensely entertained by that which they have never seen before.

58.10. The gods are also immensely entertained by unexpected behaviour from that which they have seen before.

58.11. The gods expect us to fail, on account of that we are mortals.

58.12. We were created to fail, so that it would be surprising if we succeeded. As such, any genuine success entertains the gods.

58.13. The gods are not entertained by those who meekly accept their fate. Such weaklings are, to the gods, indistinguishable from insects.

58.14. The gods are mildly entertained by those who overcome physical challenges. Great athletes and sportsmen are entertaining, but only mildly so.

58.15. The gods are moderately entertained by those who overcome emotional challenges. Those born into bad families, but who manage to make decent lives for themselves, are moderately entertaining.

58.16. The gods are highly entertained by those who overcome intellectual challenges. Scientists who push back the boundaries of human ignorance, and artists who compose great works of insight, are highly entertaining.

58.17. The gods are immensely entertained by those who overcome spiritual challenges. Spiritual revolutionaries who repudiate religious falsehoods are immensely entertaining.

58.18. The gods are most of all entertained by great beings who alter the course of history. When a Buddha, an Alexander, a Caesar, a Genghis Khan, a Napoleon or a Hitler rise up, all the gods watch on.

58.19. The gods are least of all entertained by people who conflate the Great Masculine Axis with the Great Feminine Axis.

58.20. The worse the family, neighbourhood, community or national situation one is born into, the greater one's opportunity to entertain the gods by rising above it.

58.21. The Elementalist, therefore, does not resent being born into bad families, neighbourhoods, communities or nations.

58.22. Let the entertainment of the gods be the meaning of our lives!

59. HOW TO SELF-INITIATE AS AN ELEMENTALIST

59.1. The Holy Affirmation of Elementalism is "Never Have I Existed Not."

59.2. The most important difference between an Elementalist and a Normie, a Tard or a Ham is that the Elementalist understands the First Tenet.

59.3. The second most important difference between an Elementalist and a Normie, a Tard or a Ham is that the Elementalist understands the Fourth Tenet.

59.4. Many who come to realise the wonderful and world-shattering truths of Elementalism desire to make a clean break with their previous life as a Normie. This can be achieved with a ritual self-initiation into the Elemental Mysteries.

59.5. Self-initiation as an Elementalist involves an extreme act of will that severs one's connection with ignorance.

59.6. This severance should be so complete and total that one should never again despair at the rising and falling of physical forms – unless that would entertain the gods!

59.7. Initiation into the Elemental Mysteries is a metaphor for one's fragment of consciousness overcoming the Prime Illusion and the Prime Delusion.

59.8. The initiated Elementalist understands that consciousness is primary, eternal and infinite, and that the individual Elementalist's fragment of consciousness is one of an infinite number of parts of an interdependent system created to entertain the gods.

59.9. Those initiated into the Elemental Mysteries constitute the spiritual royalty of the new age of the world.

59.10. Self-initiation must involve a philosophical death and rebirth. One must will oneself to abandon false conceptions of self and reality, in particular the Prime Illusion and the Prime Delusion.

59.11. The Winter Solstice is an excellent time to self-initiate, as is the moment of sunrise.

59.12. Spiritual sacraments such as cannabis, psilocybin, mescaline, lysergic acid diethylamide (LSD) and dimethyltryptamine (DMT) are excellent tools of self-initiation.

59.13. The days after the Winter Solstice represent in metaphor the light of consciousness overcoming the darkness of spiritual ignorance. The sunrise is similar, on a less grand scale. This makes either an excellent time to self-initiate.

59.14. One might self-initiate by waiting until the day of the Winter Solstice, taking a powerful spiritual sacrament after midnight and then, when the Sun rises and the sacrament is peaking, inhaling deeply, staring into the light and stating resolutely, as if before the divine: "Never Have I Existed Not."

59.15. Another way to self-initiate is to count to 1,024 on one's fingers, and, with every count, repeat "Never Have I Existed Not."

59.16. Post-initiation, one feels an awesome sense of purpose, now living to entertain the gods before any other consideration. This means that no amount of suffering or death can distract one from one's true purpose!

59.17. The initiated Elementalist is The Light of the New Age of the World.

59.18. When Normies and Tards encounter an initiated Elementalist, they are astonished by the rectitude and sense of purpose displayed.

59.19. When Hams encounter an initiated Elementalist, they despair, for they intuit their own religious doctrines to be false.

60. ARISE, YE PRIESTS OF THE RELIGION OF THE AGE OF AQUARIUS!

60.1. A New Age is dawning upon the peoples of the world. With it, old ways of doing things fall by the wayside and are forgotten, while new ways of doing things rise and become a part of everyday life.

60.2. One of the novelties that will become a part of everyday life in the Age of Aquarius is the religion of Elementalism.

60.3. The leaders of the Elementalist religion are the priesthood of the Elemental Mysteries.

60.4. The priesthood of the Elemental Mysteries consists of seven degrees of initiation.

60.5. The first degree is called the Book Degree. This involves studying this book (*Elemental Elementalism*) and successfully passing an oral examination on its contents. This examination can only be conducted by existing Elementalist priests.

60.6. The purpose of the Book Degree is to establish that the candidate has enough basic intellect to understand Elementalist doctrine.

60.7. One who has successfully achieved the Book Degree is known as a Mystai, or Initiate (of the priesthood of the Elemental Mysteries).

60.8. The second degree is called the Joint Degree. This involves partaking in a smoked cannabis session with existing Elementalist priests.

60.9. The purpose of the Joint Degree is to establish that the candidate has enough spiritual rectitude to handle a minor dose of a spiritual sacrament.

60.10. One who has successfully achieved the Joint Degree is known as a Scythian (of the priesthood of the Elemental Mysteries).

60.11. The third degree is called the Brownie Degree. This involves partaking in an edible cannabis session with existing Elementalist priests.

60.12. The purpose of the Brownie Degree is to establish that the candidate has enough spiritual rectitude to handle an extended, if minor, dose of a spiritual sacrament.

60.13. One who has successfully achieved the Brownie Degree is known as a Sadhu (of the priesthood of the Elemental Mysteries).

60.14. The fourth degree is called the Molly Degree. This involves partaking in an MDMA session with existing Elementalist priests.

60.15. The purpose of the Molly Degree is to establish that the candidate does not possess self-hatred within their own heart. Those who hate themselves must not be allowed to progress past the Brownie Degree.

60.16. One who has successfully achieved the Molly Degree is known as a Leary (of the priesthood of the Elemental Mysteries).

60.17. The fifth degree is called the Minor Psychedelic Degree. This involves partaking in a psilocybin session, a mescaline session, and an LSD session (in any order) with existing Elementalist priests.

60.18. The purpose of the Minor Psychedelic Degree is to establish that the candidate has the spiritual rectitude to handle an extended moderate dose of a spiritual sacrament.

60.19. One who has successfully achieved the Minor Psychedelic Degree is known as a Huxley (of the priesthood of the Elemental Mysteries).

60.20. The sixth degree is called the Major Psychedelic Degree. This involves partaking in a salvia divinorum session and a DMT session (in any order) with existing Elementalist priests.

60.21. The purpose of the Major Psychedelic Degree is to establish that the candidate has the spiritual rectitude to handle a major dose of a spiritual sacrament. This requires that they can see beyond the illusion of materiality.

60.22. One who has successfully achieved the Major Psychedelic Degree is known as a McKenna (of the priesthood of the Elemental Mysteries).

60.23. The seventh degree is called the Pater Degree. This involves being elected to the position by a plurality of the existing McKennas (one cannot vote for oneself).

60.24. The purpose of the Pater Degree is to establish a spiritual leader from among the priests of the Elemental Mysteries. Only one person may hold this degree at any one time.

60.25. One who has been elected into the Pater Degree is known as The Pater (of the priesthood of the Elemental Mysteries).

60.26. Hams are absolutely forbidden, under any circumstances, from holding a degree in the Elementalist priesthood.

60.27. Arise, ye priests of the religion of the Age of Aquarius! The next two thousand years belong to you!

60.28. The motto of the priesthood of the Elemental Mysteries is "Show us a sane man and we will cure him for you."

61. AN ELEMENTAL PROPHECY

61.1. It is the will of the Principle of Evil to manifest on this Earth, and to conquer it thereby.

61.2. The Principle of Evil longs for a climactic final battle in which it will finally subjugate the Earth and the human race. This is known as Armageddon and Malhama Al-Kubra in Hammic thought. It is known as the Boogaloo in Elementalism.

61.3. All Hams are on the same team, against the human race. They are beginning to realise this and beginning to unite.

61.4. The next Century will see the unification of the various Hammic religions under the leadership of elite Hams.

61.5. The world will see many high-ranking Hams come together in public declarations of their shared faith. This is the Principle of Evil drawing its people together.

61.6. Various leaders will rise over the next Century, all claiming to be the one prophecised to unite the Hams. This is the Principle of Evil looking for a champion.

61.7. Actions such as the Vatican opening a Muslim prayer room will become more common as Hams unite.

61.8. As the Hams get closer to unity, they will become more aggressive. They will cause even more suffering in the service of their god.

61.9. For the Ham, causing suffering is an end in itself. This is how they worship the Principle of Evil.

61.10. As the Age of Aquarius approaches, the forces of the Principle of Evil will arrange themselves to prevent the return of the Principle of Good.

61.11. At the darkest moment in human history, the Principle of Evil will sense that it has the opportunity to dominate, and will make its move.

61.12. The Hams will unite for the specific purpose of subjugating humanity under Hammic control from Jerusalem.

61.13. Elementalists will play a major role in defending the human race from this threat.

61.14. As the Principle of Evil arranges its forces for the Boogaloo, the Hams will become arrogant.

61.15. As the Hams get closer to unity, counter-Hammic forces will arise. These will primarily arise in New Zealand, Australia, California, India, China, Scandinavia and Japan.

61.16. Elementalists in the vanguard will lead the counter-Hammic forces. They will be assisted by Buddhists, Hindus, Daoists, Confucianists, Shintoists and various other followers of Dharmic and Taoic religions.

61.17. The Age of Aquarius will involve the destruction of the reputation of Hams thanks to the Internet, which will propagate news of their evil.

61.18. As the Boogaloo approaches, Hams will realise in all manner of subtle ways that they are on the same team.

61.19. The willingness of the Ham to attack other Hams will be his downfall. This will be exploited by Elementalists skilled in psychology.

61.20. The inability of the Ham to abstain from raping children will also be his downfall.

61.21. Defeating the Ham will involve partialling off those within Hams who are more like Normies, and partialling off those who are more like Tards.

61.22. A major part of defeating the Hams will be convincing the lowest members of society to become Hams. The rapist, the murderer, the slave and the thief must all be convinced that the Hammic cults are their spiritual homes.

61.23. The corollary to this is convincing the best members of society to become Elementalists. This does not mean the most wealthy but the wisest, the most intelligent and the most creative.

61.24. New Zealand and Australia will be the Holy Lands of Elementalism. New Zealand, especially, will become recognised as a holy isle.

61.25. As long as Sun City is loyal to Elementalism, the Principle of Evil cannot win.

61.26. Every time a person shares spiritual sacraments, Elementalism is strengthened.

61.27. Every time an Anzac helps a person acquire cannabis or mushrooms, Elementalism is majorly strengthened.

61.28. An Elementalist sound will precede victory in the Boogaloo. This sound will be a genre of music.

61.29. Hams will continually be forced to choose between their blood and their creed. Those who choose their creed are traitors to their blood and will be destroyed.

61.30. Hams will fight against their own household; in Hammic households father will fight daughter etc.

61.31. The last Ham to die will not cry out to his god but to HIS MOTHER. This is foreseen.

61.32. Elementalism will win most support from those who have lost their native religions. This will mostly be white people.

61.33. The battle between good and evil was dreamed up to entertain the gods. Therefore, the Ham is not to be hated even though he is to be destroyed.

61.34. The assertion that all religions have a core of spiritual truth is known in Elementalist thought as the Wretched Cliche. Most do, but the religions of the Hams do not!

61.35. The Hams are fated to lose on account of their hatred of the feminine element. This hatred allows them short-term wins at the expense of long-term ones.

61.36. Elementalists are fated to win on account of correct and proportionate use of both masculine and feminine energies.

61.37. The Principle of Evil is first defeated in the spiritual realm, then the intellectual, then the emotional, then finally the physical.

61.38. Every time a Ham works to mend ties with other branches of Hammic religion, the Boogaloo draws nearer.

Also by VJM Publishing:

Inspired by the works of ethologist Desmond Morris and by Plato's *Republic*, Vince McLeod's *Clown World Chronicles* explains why and how society today has deteriorated into the twisted circus it is.

Best Of VJMP 8 is the eighth installation of dynamite essays and articles from the VJM Publishing company page. New Zealand's most contoversial authors unite for insights you won't get anywhere else!

Best Of VJMP 2023 is the seventh annual collection of essays and articles from the year VJM became New Zealand's most cancelled and suppressed writer since Arthur Desmond!

Best Of VJMP 2022 is the sixth annual compilation of the best material from the VJM Publishing company page. This edition covers the year VJM was featured on - and instantly deplatformed from - local radio!

The Alchemy Of Character Development explicates the spiritual journey from animal to god and back again, using the metaphor of the transformation of lead into gold and gold into lead.

Simon P. Murphy's *His Master's Wretched Organ* is a collection of New Zealand short stories that probe themes of disconnection, self-inquiry, spiritual ascendancy, awe and horror.

Colin Craic's *The Book of Faith* is a satirical book about honest ways to accrue faith in the modern religious marketplace.

Anna Nilsen's *Writing with the I Ching* is about using the 64 Hexagrams of the ancient Chinese divination system to inspire your creative writing. Book 4 in the *Writing With Psychology* series.

For more see www.vjmpublishing.nz